the
burning
ones

Igniting and fuelling a passion for Jesus

Steve Uppal

RIVER
PUBLISHING

River Publishing & Media Ltd
Barham Court
Teston
Maidstone
Kent
ME18 5BZ
United Kingdom

info@river-publishing.co.uk

ISBN 978-1-908393-30-2
Printed in the USA by Edwards Brothers Malloy
Cover design by www.SpiffingCovers.com

Contents

What Others Are Saying...

"Steve's words are solidly based in Scripture and given context by the wise words of passionate pioneers of Church history. The danger of a passionate book is that it can fuel the fires of mavericks, if read wrongly. Steve navigates this possibility with great wisdom and writes, 'This is not a move of God just for leaders or to create a Christian elite.' It would be great if we could all be infected by the holy virus of this book!" **Stuart Bell, Leader of the Ground Level Network, Senior Leader of New Life Lincoln.**

"Too many have missed the opportunity to excel in their full potential for God because they fail to understand what it means to dwell in the secret place of the Most High ... Enjoy the book and rediscover your passion for Jesus." **David L'Herroux, Managing Director, UCB**

"The Lord has given Steve Uppal a strong message for the United Kingdom and beyond. I urge you to read this book prayerfully and discern the Lord's call to you expressed in these pages. This book has the potential to be a fire-starter in your life." **Bob Sorge, author, oasishouse.com**

"Steve's passion is that a successful future does not depend on getting God on our agenda, but recalibrating our lives so that we are on His. Steve is not a theoretician. What he is inviting us to encounter has been worked out in local church as well as in his own life. *The Burning Ones* is truth on fire." **John Glass, Elim General Superintendent**

"Steve's own commitment and passion for Jesus come across clearly and is sure to impact any reader – it is contagious! I could not put this book down once I'd started - you have been warned!" **Ram Gidomal, Chairman of the Lausanne Movement**

"An inspiring, sobering book, challenging us to live in a place of intimacy with the One who gave His all for us. It is a book you will pick up time and time again as you seek to keep your heart aflame." **Manoj Raithatha, National Co-ordinator of South Asian Forum, Director of Instant Apostle Publishing House**

"Steve Uppal gives each honest reader a path to a great and forgotten truth about revival: it starts in your heart first. I hope you will take time out of your busy life and give this book a heartfelt read. It could be the book that helps you make the grand step toward the revival you are looking for." **Roberts Liardon, author of God's Generals**

"A much-needed book by a practitioner who has a fire and passion for Jesus. This could be one of your best reads this year." **John Partington, National Leader Assemblies of God GB**

"Ignatius would end his sermons by saying, 'Let's go out and set the world alight.' This book sets out to do the same. It all flows from a revolutionary encounter with Jesus that will ignite us with the same passion." **Roy Crowne, Executive Director HOPE**

"Not for the faint-hearted, but a rousing rally call to take God's word seriously and not to rest on our laurels. Filled with prophetic bite; a stirring read." **Steve Clifford, General Director, Evangelical Alliance**

Acknowledgements

Thanks to my beautiful wife of 16 years for her encouragement and for releasing me to have the time to write this book. Also to Bethany, Sophia, Joel and Judah, you all showed so much excitement and enthusiasm while Daddy was writing.

I have been part of the All Nations family for more than 20 years and have had the privilege of bringing the senior lead for the last 12 years. Being a part of this community has taught me so very much. Your excitement for me to write was overwhelming. I am sure I would not be the person I am today without the All Nations Family. Thank you all for your friendship, love and continued encouragement. Our best days are ahead!

When asked why so many thousands would come to listen to him, John Wesley said, I set myself on fire and the world comes to watch me burn!

Introduction

My desire is that through this book the Lord will both ignite and fuel a passion for Jesus in you. We are living in the last days and an army is being roused (the theme of my first book *Rousing the Warriors*) and also prepared for the coming battles and clashes with darkness. These are sobering days for people who take the things of God seriously and not casually.

Isaiah 60:1-2 says,

"Arise, shine, for your light has come, and the glory of the Lord rises upon you. See, darkness covers the earth and thick darkness is over the peoples, but the Lord rises upon you and his glory appears over you."

This prophetic scripture, written more than two and a half thousand years ago, is relevant for these and the coming days. My prayer is that the message of this book will help you to Arise and Shine to your fullest potential. There are many things I could have written about and some may have been more acceptable to the wider Church. But I have a conviction that this book is a message that the Body of Christ needs to hear. I believe I am writing in response to the leading of the Holy Spirit.

There are two things you will notice throughout this book. Firstly, there are many scripture references – some quoted in full and others just referred to. I encourage you to read them all carefully with an open heart. I am aware some readers have a habit of skipping over the scripture quotations in books and focusing only on the words of the author. Please don't do this! Instead let the Word do it's work in you.

Secondly, I quote quite extensively from "Burning Ones" in history. I make no apology for this, because I firmly believe they will be of help to you and, as they did for me, that they will set your heart on fire. Throughout my life I have walked with the giants of the past and found comfort and like-minded friends there. I have also been broken by their lives and commitment and stirred to serve Jesus more wholeheartedly. I am trusting the same will happen for you as you read their words in this book.

There is a generation rising of the same calibre as the giants of the past – some who, I believe, will go further and achieve more for the Kingdom of God than their predecessors. Remember, we are not in competition with them, but we learn from their lives in order to see further and accomplish great things in our day. Our beginnings may yet be small, but I am convinced that the Lord saves His best wine till last and we will see mighty warriors coming forth in these days.

My efforts in writing this book leave me feeling like the boy with five small loaves and two small fish facing a crowd of more than 5,000 men, plus women and children. My prayer is that God will take the little I have to offer and feed and satisfy the hungry.

Steve Uppal

You yourselves are our letter, written on our hearts, known and read by everybody. You show that you are a letter from Christ, the result of our ministry, written not with ink but with the Spirit of the living God, not on tablets of stone but on tablets of human hearts.
(2 Corinthians 3:2-3)

These things happened to them as examples and were written down... for us, on whom the fulfillment of the ages has come.
(1 Corinthians 10:11)

1
My Story

It was February 1995. I sat on the floor feeling like something was really wrong, but I didn't know what. I felt empty, as though hope was slipping through my fingers, but I was helpless to do anything about it. Whereas once I felt strong, buoyant and filled with energy, now I felt the opposite. The clarity of mind I normally lived with seemed to have deserted me and now I was filled with confusion; the hope of better days and new opportunities had gone.

I couldn't clearly articulate what I was feeling or why, so I just ignored the feelings, hoping that things would soon somehow change. I had felt this a number of times in the last few weeks ... or was it months? I could normally shake it off and carry on with my busy schedule, serving the Lord, preaching and travelling. Little did I realise the severity of what was going on inside me.

I was 20 years old and in full-time ministry, busy travelling and preaching. In many ways I was living my dream. Let me give you the back story.

I was born into a Sikh family. I was only 5 weeks old when my parents heard the awesome news about Jesus Christ and how He loved them, died for them and came back to life by God's divine power. They discovered that this same Jesus offered them eternal life. My parents readily committed their lives to Christ in May 1974. So I had the privilege of being raised by Christian parents who modelled for me a love and respect for God and His Word. They weren't your normal "Sunday" Christians, but radical, devoted followers of Jesus, devouring every book about Him, memorising portions of the Bible, meeting with other believers regularly and attending every meeting they could possibly get to. I grew up in that environment. I didn't know any different. To me, God was real. He was big and He deserved my best.

I was only 5 years old when I made my very own personal commitment to Christ. This is how it happened. I remember lying in bed one evening feeling very alone and scared. We lived in the same house as my grandparents, uncle and aunties and their families (not uncommon in the 70's). No one else was upstairs and yet when my head touched the pillow I could hear footsteps coming down the hall. Images of the Sikh gurus with the orange robes tormented my mind (there were pictures of them scattered around our home, as only my parents were Christians). I would sit up and the sound of the footsteps would stop. Little did I know, as a naive five-year old that it was actually the sound of my own heart beating that I could hear. Eventually,

I slipped out of bed, got onto my knees and asked Jesus to come into my life and take away this fear.

My dad had told me that any time I wanted or needed God I could call on Him and He would answer. There and then I promised to serve Him and love Him all my days. It was simple, but it was heartfelt and sincere.

Pretty much straight away I developed a hunger for spiritual things. My dad had been teaching me simple Bible verses since I could speak. He also had a small library of Christian books and from the age of about seven I was drawn to these. I was also drawn to listen to the teaching cassettes he had collected, of preachers from all over the world teaching the Bible. I seemed to have an unquenchable hunger for the things of God and the older I got, the hungrier I became, continually devouring books from my Dad's bookshelf. I would also urge Dad to take me with him to the meetings he would go to whenever traveling preachers were in town or somewhere nearby.

I was required by my parents to develop the habit of reading the Bible every day. Sometimes this was a chore, as I couldn't always understand what I was reading, but nevertheless it was done.

When I was eight years old I was taken to a special service for young people in the nearby city of Birmingham. It was here that I heard a message about being filled with the Holy Spirit and the gift of tongues being given, just as it had been for the early disciples in Acts 2. And that is exactly what happened to me that very night. I was baptised in the Holy Spirit and spoke with other tongues.

Another significant moment came when I was eleven. I accompanied my Dad to a series of special meetings on demonology! Yes, you read it right. I was the only young person at these Bible studies, but was so hungry to learn about the spiritual world. I had mixture of excitement and fear each week as we attended these meetings and a thousand questions for my Dad afterwards. During the third week of these meetings the preacher, who was from another part of the UK, stopped halfway through his message, pointed at me and asked me to come out. He told me that since I had come into the room, the Holy Spirit had been urging him to pray and prophesy over me. He had thought it best to leave it until the end of the meeting, but the prompting of the Spirit had intensified until he had to obey. He then told me that the Lord had called and chosen me and that I would travel the world preaching and teaching for Jesus. He said that wherever I went around the world evil spirits would be afraid, because I would come in Jesus' name and with His power. He then gave me some scripture and charged me to live a clean, holy life and to devour God's Word with all my heart.

I think the Lord orchestrated things to happen this way so that these words would stay with me and be impressed upon me. Needless to say, this event left an indelible mark on me and it was a significant turning point in my spiritual life.

As an eleven-year old I fully expected invitations to begin

coming in from all over the world. The next three weeks I checked the post every morning to see if there were any invitations (there were none). I also carried my Bible with me everywhere and began to read it like I never had before. I took it with me to school and every lunch and break time I would open it up and read. I had no shame or embarrassment, just a love for God.

The next milestone came two years later, aged thirteen. Some of my passion for God had waned. No preaching invitations had come and the prophetic word I had received two years earlier seemed like it had fired blanks. Life was mundane and God didn't seem very close either. At that young age I didn't understand that between the "promise" and the "promised land" there is nearly always a wilderness. Often that period of time is for the preparation of the person to be able to handle the promise that is coming. But many people lose their way during this wilderness period.

I was becoming like many teenagers around me at school. I attended church, still read my Bible and lived an "okay" life on the outside. But on the inside, I was beginning to be drawn towards other things, the things of this world.

I did not realise it, but everything was about to change. I attended a Christian camp that summer and encountered God in a way that I had never previously known. The preacher challenged us to live the Christian life in action and not only in name. I publicly stood and responded to the altar call.

Afterwards, I remember my heart feeling like it was on fire, alive with God's love. I felt His presence pulsating through my very being and left that evening service to be alone with God, walking in the moonlit fields nearby, pouring out my affections to Him. I was His and He was mine and that was all that mattered. I didn't want to be "normal" any more. I felt awakened for the first time in my life and Jesus' joy filled my heart to overflowing. In this moment everything seemed to make sense: I was born to know Him and have Him live inside of me.

Everything seemed different after that night. I had a joy and excitement bubbling up within me that I had never known before. I was drawn to the Bible, Christian books, audio messages. I couldn't wait for Sundays to be in church, praise and worship God again with others and to listen to the preacher. It didn't really matter what songs were sung or who the preacher was. I always felt like God was there just to meet with me and speak to me. I was in my own personal revival.

The summer holidays were soon over and school began again. It had been a long six-week break and a lot had happened in me during that time. As I got back into school and saw my old friends, there was a battle within me. Should I tell them what had happened? How was I supposed to live? Should my language be different? What about the jokes we were telling or the way we answered back to some of our teachers?

You see, in the previous term I had developed a small group of friends and we were cheeky, rude, and my language had started slipping into profanities (although only at school). For the first week or so I tried to fit in with the way things used to be, but it was no good, it wasn't me any more and I couldn't do it. I finally spoke up during one lunch hour and told my friends what had happened to me over the summer – how I had encountered God and made a commitment to live the Christian life, not just to wear the label "Christian". I went on and expressed that my language, humor and attitude all had to fall in line with that new commitment and that I was finding it really difficult to do this while keeping their company. They looked at me with blank stares. I assured them that it wasn't because of them, but because of me. I had changed. Then I quietly walked away.

That led to almost two years of pretty much being on my own in school. I used my breaks and lunch hours to read my Bible, memorise scripture and sometimes find a quiet place to pray. I shared my faith with as many people as I possibly could. It was in these early months that another school friend and I struck up a friendship. He came from a traditional Christian home, but now our Christianity took on a whole new passion and fervour. We didn't see each other much in school, but met regularly outside. I had found a friend with the same fire and excitement for Jesus. We fueled each other's passion.

Slowly, one by one, the number of friends I had began to grow and within a few short weeks there were about 10 young men meeting in my home every Tuesday evening.

We would worship together, I would preach, and then we would pray. I used to set a scripture memory verse each week for them, typing every little card on an old typewriter. I would set crazy challenges like reading the New Testament through in two weeks or the four gospels four times in four weeks. At times I challenged everyone in the group not to watch any TV for a given period in order to give more of our time to reading the Bible. We gave ourselves to half-night and all-night prayer sessions. We prayed for our school friends, for revival and for anything else we could think of.

All this took place in my parents' home. There was always plenty of fun, laughter, fighting and eating – as you might expect from teenage boys.

After about a year of meeting like this every week, we started to feel the Lord speaking to us, encouraging us to reach out to other young people. We were already committed to praying for our school friends, but we had a leading to begin a small ministry that could reach out to others. It began when my Youth Pastor asked if I would bring this small group to take a youth service at my local church. I was delighted to accept.

We came up with some drama, one of the lads could sing, I encouraged another to begin to rap and I would preach. We practiced the material again and again until it was perfect. I wanted us to do the best we possibly could. We prayed fervently for that youth service in the preceding weeks. We got there early on that Friday so we could pray again before the service. I knew we needed God to show up and change lives.

And then we poured out our hearts in front of 15-20 young

people. If I am honest, I don't fully remember everything about that evening, but it opened up another invitation to a different youth group and that opened up a few more. Before we knew it the diary was being filled up through youth groups in our area asking us to come and minister to them.

We called ourselves Christian Warriors and gave ourselves the strapline, "The Power of Love". This eventually became "Ambassadors for Christ". Our messages were always fiery and challenging, calling young people to an all-out commitment in service to Christ.

There were no holds barred, the gospel was preached, and full commitment to Christ asked for.

We bought the same black tops from a local clothing shop and one of the young men created a logo which he hand painted onto each shirt. Now we had a uniform and a logo. I remember thinking that we needed our own sound system. The cassette player we took to youth services was okay, but limited. Many churches at that time didn't have good PA systems. So we began to pray and ask the Lord to help us with this. We even started putting our own money together each week, saving towards the ministry expenses we incurred. We didn't have much, but it did start building up.

I still remember the youth meeting in Gornal, Dudley, where we received a small gift from the youth funds for ministering and then the youth leader and his wife gave us a personal gift of £100 towards purchasing a sound system. I had never known so much money to be given and was taken aback. I thanked them profusely and celebrated with the team at God's provision and goodness. It was only a short while later, with a few hundred pounds, that three of us took the train to the nearby city of Birmingham to see what our money would buy us. We came back with a small amplifier that had 4 inputs, two speakers, two microphones and some leads. We carried it by hand on the train and then by bus back to my home. We wasted no time setting it up in the garden and blasting out our songs.

Little by little we saw God grow our influence, open more doors and providing more resources. Soon we were travelling further a field and sometimes for a weekend or even a few days. During our half term breaks we were used for schools work in other localities. We were always dependent on parents or kind church members who were sympathetic to our cause for transport. Brochures were designed by hand and printed, a regular newsletter and partner base began. Everything was pretty much done by hand, since few people possessed computers at this time. Eight hundred address, all written out by hand each month! All this was done on evenings and weekends since we were still at school during the day.

Back at school new friendships began to form. I now felt much stronger so as not to be swayed in my faith by others, but rather to be an influence to them. I also began a Christian Union at school. It started with just a handful of people, but it wasn't long before numbers grew and we would have up to forty or so attending each week. We then moved from having a weekly meeting on a Friday to meeting daily during one of our break times to pray for the school and its students. We produced a fortnightly magazine for the Christian Union and organised day trips to Christian youth events. We witnessed many people make commitments to Christ and many others who were weak in their faith become strong and bold. (Interestingly some of those we prayed for and witnessed to have become Christians 15-20 years later and are now in my church!)

During this season I was personally being pulled closer to the Lord. I loved reading the biographies of great Christians. I read of George Muller, Smith Wigglesworth and Hudson Taylor. I read of the Welsh Revival, the Indonesian Revival, and others.

These stories and lives left a deep desire and hunger in me for more of the Lord. I wanted Him. I wanted to do more for Him. I knew if He could use those other people that I too could be a candidate. For a whole season during these years I gave myself to fasting every Monday, Wednesday and Friday (much to the horror of my mother). I would meet with one of my friends (the first friend who joined the Christian Warriors) at 6.00am on midweek mornings to pray for our school. We later changed to meet three times a week.

We would also set each other scripture memory challenges, setting out to memorise whole passages and even entire chapters of the Bible. As a team we prayed each week in our Tuesday meetings and would also spend around an hour in prayer before we began any ministry service we were invited to. All of these things caused us to encounter God and grow in Him, becoming stronger in the Lord.

* * *

Now fast forward a little and let's retun to the twenty-year old sitting on the floor feeling hopeless. What had happened? By twenty the ministry had become a machine that needed to be kept in motion. I had experienced some painful relational disappointments with team members leaving. Life was very, very busy and as a result I had started to neglect my walk with Jesus. I thought I knew what to do and how to do it, so we prayed less and I fasted less. I hadn't realised this had happened. It was the pressure all around me. Something had to give and my time with Jesus gave way to the busyness. It's a classic mistake made by many and I fell for it.

My focus shifted. Whereas before my confidence was in God alone and I was reliant on His ability to do things, now I had allowed myself to become confident in my own abilities. I had gained some experience and thought I knew what I was doing. I had begun to believe the hype others spoke about me.

But whilst I was enjoying the busy schedule of ministry, I was actually neglecting the One for whose glory it was all being done. Having visited many churches and conducted hundreds of meetings, I was no longer ministering from the overflow of a heart on fire. I was now a "professional" who understood how things worked.

Needless to say, the Lord rescued me, but not before more breaking of my self and pride. It has been a process over the years and I still surprise myself as to how quickly I can forget these lessons and begin to repeat them. What was the remedy? Returning to my first love and a total dependence upon God; to have my heart healed and set on fire again, and to learn how to keep that fire burning.

I tell my story because I believe that in it there may be echoes of your story – the dreams, the life, the hopes, and perhaps the resignation of having to live a "normal" life because of many disappointments.

But there should be no "normal", not for those in whom the Creator of the universe lives. It is time to break the lies of the enemy and the yoke put on us by other people's expectations.

It is time for dreams to be awakened again. God is raising, calling a Company of Burning Hearts. Almost 20 years since the story above, I am more on fire now than ever before. I have had to fight the constant pressure of other people's expectations of what ministry should be like, what church should be like and so on.

Since those days I have learnt that my number one reason for existing is to glorify God through my life. As one preacher put it, "God is most glorified in me when I am most satisfied in Him." I am to know Him enjoy Him above all else.

Let hope arise in you.

Your story is not over. It's not too late.

This book has found it's way into your hands for a reason. The Father is calling you.

IGNITING THE FLAME

- Take some time to look back over your life and identify those times when God met with you or spoke specific things into your life. He wants you to have a fresh encounter with Him today – right now.

- What things has God said to you about your life? It's time to kindle that flame that He has placed inside you; to reconnect with His destiny for you. God has an amazing adventure prepared just for you. It's time to begin to get passionate about it.

Above all, George Fox excelled in prayer. The inwardness and weight of his spirit, the reverence and solemnity of his address and behaviour, and the fewness and fulness of his words have often struck even strangers with admiration, as they were used to reach others with consolation. The most awful, living, reverend frame I ever felt or beheld, I must say, was the prayer of George Fox. And truly it was a testimony. He knew and lived nearer to the Lord than other men, for they that know Him most will see most reason to approach Him with reverence and fear.

– William Penn

2
A Company of Burning Hearts

The title of this book came out of two ministry experiences I had a few years ago. Please allow me to share both with you. The first took place in May 2010. I preached in a small church in North Wales and after preaching, as I began praying for people, the presence of God was strong and weighty. After I had finished ministering to the people three ladies came forward and said, "Please pray for us." One had been in the meeting and was so touched by the Lord that she went and got two of her friends who weren't at the meeting to come and receive ministry. They were hungry, very hungry, for Jesus and wanted to encounter Him afresh. It was clear that these women had been cultivating a desire and hunger for Jesus in their private lives. The Lord gave me a picture of some dry cracked earth that was longing for rain to fall upon it. I knew it represented these ladies. As we stood in a circle together and I began to pray, the weightiness of

God's presence increased and all of us had powerful encounters with Him for whom we were created. I was very touched by the hunger I witnessed in these women. I felt there was something special about them. But not only them, I had a sense that the Lord was stirring many people in the UK and all over the world in a similar way.

As I walked away the Lord spoke clearly into my heart: "I am raising a company of burning hearts." Though I did not hear an audible voice, I felt the significance of the phrase the Holy Spirit had just quickened to me. *A Company of Burning Hearts*. It reverberated through me and I felt the Lord saying that He has many whose hearts are being set aflame for Jesus. There are also those who have a deep yearning within them, knowing that there must be more than they currently live in, though they have not yet experienced it. They feel like ground that is dry, cracked and longing for the rains of His presence to fall down and saturate them.

The Lord is answering this heart thirst and hunger. It is not an accident that this book is in your hands. You are being "set up" for a life-changing encounter. You do not have to live with a dry, cold heart. You were created to carry the very presence of the God within you.

Luke 24 tells us the story of two disciples whose hearts were heavy and broken because they had witnessed Jesus killed upon the cross. All their hopes and dreams had been placed upon Him, yet they had seen Him die. With His death their dreams and aspirations were also dealt a fatal blow.

But as they walked from Jerusalem to Emmaus, a stranger joined them. They walked 7 miles with Jesus, not knowing it was Him. He spoke to them from the Scriptures, explaining many things to them. Afterwards, when their eyes were opened, they realised it was Jesus and then He disappeared. They said to each other, *"Did not our hearts burn within us when he talked to us"* (Luke 24:32)

Your heart was created to burn, to be aflame, to be alive, overflowing with the radiating glory of His divine presence. Adam and Eve lived in the atmosphere of that glory. Enoch walked so closely with God that he never experienced death, but was translated from this earthly realm to heaven. Humans were created to house the Divine. To live in communion with our Maker is not a pipe-dream. Because of the work of Jesus on the cross it can be a reality now. We have settled for way below God's best, allowing our lives to be lived in mediocrity and often captivated by temporal things. Blaise Pascal said,

"There is a God-shaped vacuum in the heart of every man which cannot be filled by any created thing, but only by God, the Creator, made known through Jesus."

You are not complete until that void is filled and only His tangible glory can fill it. We have fallen into a trap of making converts rather than following Jesus' command to make disciples. Disciples are those who imitate their Master, live with Him, and learn from Him to become just like Him. They walk with

Him each and every day in a real, living, dynamic relationship.

"Do you not know that your body is a temple of the Holy Spirit, who is in you, whom you have received from God? You are not your own." (1 Corinthians 6:19)

Our bodies are meant to house God. It's where the Holy Spirit lives and takes up residence. You and I are dwelling places for Him. This is not only an amazing truth, it can be the reality for you, even beginning today.

The second ministry experience I had was similar to the first. I preached in a church in the south of England and had offered to pray with people. Probably 50-75 people had responded and I was slowly making my way down the line. Again, the presence of God was strong and many people were meeting with their Lord and Saviour in a new way. I am so happy that the Holy Spirit lives in me and I get to work with Him. It makes life fun and adventurous. As I moved along the line of people, I moved to place my hands on the head of the next person and suddenly felt a sober stillness come over me. I'm not sure exactly how to describe it, but I felt I couldn't lay hands on the person in front of me. She was a young girl, maybe 19-20 years old. She stood with her eyes closed and tears streaming down her face. I felt the Lord speak into my heart and say, "She is one of my Holy Ones." I felt the Lord show me this girl in her secret place with Him. She was a pursuer of God, fasting, praying, weeping, longing only for Him. She had chosen to turn away from the things this world would use to entice her away from her one true love. That evening I encountered three such people. I felt humbled and also privileged to pray with them. I left very aware that a special Company of Burning Ones was being summoned.

I am convinced that there is a whole army of these people across the earth. They may not be famous, they come from all walks of life, but they are the "Holy Ones" that Enoch prophesied about.

"Enoch, the seventh from Adam, prophesied about these men: 'See, the Lord is coming with thousands upon thousands of his holy ones to judge everyone...'" (Jude 14)

We are seeing the fulfillment of that prophecy in these days. I am not speaking of something that is yet to happen, it has begun already. Men, women and children have been responding to the drawing of the Holy Spirit. We may not see it fully yet, but when the fullness of time comes we will see the work of the Lord. These Holy ones will manifest the power and nature of Jesus. They will be from all walks of life, young and old. Their lives, their words, the manifestations of the Kingdom will both convict and save, pointing people to Jesus. These are tremendous days on the earth. Don't let them pass you by. I believe the invitation to join this Company is open to all who have ears to hear what the Spirit is saying to the Church. You can be a part of this movement and should be a part.

Forerunners

I have always been attracted to those in history who were

marked by heaven. Reformers like John Wesley and William Booth, Revivalists like Evan Roberts, Charles Finney. Healing Evangelists like Smith Wigglesworth and Kathryn Kuhlman or Pastors like George Muller and Robert Murray McCheyne.

There are so many more I could mention, but one thing is true about them all: they were marked by heaven and all of them bore the fruit in their lives of carrying God's power and presence, seeing the world around them changed. Some moved in outstanding miracles and others brought earnest works of God to communities, resulting in transformed, villages, towns and cities. Without exception they each had a deep desire and love for Jesus that they cultivated and nurtured.

Their hearts were literally aflame with Him.

Today we read and tell their stories and are fascinated by the fruit of their lives. I too, love to read and speak about what the Lord did through His mighty servants. I think this is good because it stirs faith and hunger in us. But I have felt the Lord say to me that they were *forerunners.* There was often just one or two of them, perhaps a handful, in a generation. A forerunner is someone who goes ahead or is sent in advance to announce the coming of someone or something that will follow. John the baptist was a forerunner for Christ. He announced His coming. His life was given to prepare for the coming of the Messiah.

Those I have mentioned above were forerunners. Their lives were a prophetic sign of many more to come like them. But I believe that for the first time, rather than there being just a few in our generation, there will be countless hundreds, even thousands, walking in the manifest power of God. I believe this to my very core and I am living for this. Some (like Smith Wigglesworth in 1947) have prophesied about the day we are in and how the Lord will move in revival power.

Smith Wigglesworth's 1947 Prophecy

Two Distinct Moves

"During the next few decades there will be two distinct moves of the Holy Spirit across the Church in Great Britain. The first move will affect every church that is open to receive it and will be characterised by a restoration of the baptism and gifts of the Holy Spirit. The second move of the Holy Spirit will result in people leaving historic churches and planting new churches. In the duration of each of these moves, the people who are involved will say 'This is the great revival.' But the Lord says, 'No, neither is this the great revival, but both are steps towards it.'

Word and Spirit

When the new church phase is on the wane, there will be evidenced in the churches something that has not been seen before: a coming together of those with an emphasis on the Word and those with an emphasis on the Spirit.

When the Word and the Spirit come together, there will be the biggest movement of the Holy Spirit that the nation, and indeed the world, has ever seen. It will mark the beginning of a revival that will eclipse anything that has been witnessed within these shores, even the Wesleyan and the Welsh revivals of former years. The outpouring of God's Spirit will flow over from the UK to the mainland of Europe, and from there will begin a missionary move to the ends of the earth."

This prophetic word, given more than 60 years ago, is upon us today! We must fight the fear and depression that covers much of the earth and has crept into the Church and rise up to see and hear what the Lord is doing. Cynicism and doubt have eaten away at many in the Church, until there is little or no faith in God and His Word. Jesus said about the these last days, *"When the Son of Man comes will he find faith on the earth"* (Luke 18:8). Whenever I read these words I always say, "Lord, find it in me."

One of the significant things about this time we are in and the Company of Burning Hearts is the fact they they will be both clergy and laity. This is not a move of God for leaders or to create a Christian elite. We will see people in everyday jobs and situations walking in the weighty, undeniable power of God. Some have referred to them as a nameless, faceless army, meaning that they won't be people with large churches, TV ministeries or some great following. They will not be building a platform selfishly for themselves, but will point to Jesus in all things. He is turning His Body inside out and it is the day of the Church. I am not saying that leaders won't be used, but that it is not exclusively for leaders. This is for all believers.

Arise and Shine

"Arise, shine, for your light has come,
and the glory of the Lord rises upon you.
See, darkness covers the earth
and thick darkness is over the peoples,
but the Lord rises upon you
and his glory appears over you." (Isaiah 6:1-2)

I say to you Arise, your light has come. Yes, darkness covers the earth, but the Lord appears over you and His glory rises upon you. It is your time to shine brightly. You were born for this very purpose. We have settled for a nice, palatable brand of Christianity that has been lukewarm, predictable and disgusting to God. Through the remainder of this book I want to inspire and stir faith in you to believe that you can be one of the people who refuse to settle for this. I will go as far as to say that God wants you to be a "Burning One". It is your calling and destiny. You are not reading this book by accident. This has been the deep cry of your heart. Perhaps you have not been able to articulate it, but the deep of God is calling to the deep within you. Eternity is set in the hearts of men (Ecclesiastes 3:11).

"Deep calls to deep in the roar of your waterfalls; all your waves and breakers have swept over me." (Psalm 42:8)

I also want to put real tools in your hand to enable you to know how to activate and fuel these things in your life. Inspiration alone will not bring lasting change in us. But understanding the ways of the Kingdom and conforming our lives to those ways will transform us. Ultimately, Jesus is the transformation we are looking for. My prayer is that your heart will be set aflame and that you will have knowledge of how to keep the fire burning. Purpose to open your heart and hear the voice of the Holy Spirit through these pages. Make a commitment to read carefully and to prayerfully apply the challenges you feel in your Spirit.

IGNITING THE FLAME

- You don't have to be specially qualified to belong to the company of burning hearts that God is raising up. Allow some time for this truth to soak into your soul. God is calling you, personally, to be one of the army of His "Holy Ones".

- Make a habit of praying each day and asking God to help your desires to come into alignment with His desires; your will with His will. As you do, you will experience an increasing awareness of His peace in your life and you will also begin to hear His voice more clearly.

The Obstacle of Dullness

We have lost our astonishment. The Good News is no longer good news, it is okay news. Christianity is no longer life changing, it is life enhancing. Jesus doesn't change people into wild-eyed radicals any more, He changes them into 'nice people.'

If Christianity is simply about being nice, I'm not interested. What happened to radical Christianity that turned the world upside-down? What happened to the category-smashing, life-threatening, anti-institutional gospel that spread through the 1st century like wildfire and was considered (by those in power) dangerous? What happened to the kind of Christians whose hearts were on fire, who had no fear, who spoke the truth no matter what the consequence, who made the world uncomfortable, who were willing to follow Jesus wherever He went? What happened to the kind of Christians who were filled with passion and gratitude, and who every day were unable to get over the grace of God?

I'm ready for a Christianity that ruins my life, that captures my heart and makes me uncomfortable. I want to be filled with an astonishment which is so captivating that I am considered wild and unpredictable and...well...dangerous. Yes, I want to be 'dangerous' to a dull and boring religion. I want a faith that is considered dangerous by our predictable and monotonous culture.

- Michael Yaconnelli, Dangerous Wonder

3
Highly Flammable

You have a choice about how you choose to live your life. You can live in a cold, apathetic way, just drifting from one day to the next or you can know the hot, fiery passion and love of God burning in your heart and flowing through your veins. We shouldn't leave the direction of our life to chance. There are steps we can take to fuel the fire. In this chapter I want to help you understand how to make your life highly flammable. Here we will look briefly at a number of points and then expand on them a little more throughout the remainder of this book.

Allow me to pull out some relevant lessons from a very well known Old Testament story. It is a true story, recounting events that actually took place. But for us it is also a parable – a story with a greater meaning.

"Then Elijah said to all the people, 'Come here to me.' They came to him, and he repaired the altar of the Lord, which was in ruins. Elijah took twelve stones, one for each of the tribes descended from Jacob, to whom the word of the Lord had come,

saying, 'Your name shall be Israel.' With the stones he built an altar in the name of the Lord, and he dug a trench around it large enough to hold two seahs of seed. He arranged the wood, cut the bull into pieces and laid it on the wood. Then he said to them, 'Fill four large jars with water and pour it on the offering and on the wood.' 'Do it again,' he said, and they did it again. 'Do it a third time,' he ordered, and they did it the third time. The water ran down around the altar and even filled the trench.

At the time of sacrifice, the prophet Elijah stepped forward and prayed: 'O Lord, God of Abraham, Isaac and Israel, let it be known today that you are God in Israel and that I am your servant and have done all these things at your command. Answer me, O Lord, answer me, so these people will know that you, O Lord, are God, and that you are turning their hearts back again.' Then the fire of the Lord fell and burned up the sacrifice, the wood, the stones and the soil, and also licked up the water in the trench." (1 Kings 18:30-38)

Come here to me...

Elijah pulled people into his proximity. He wanted them to see what God was about to do. He wanted this event to be a real challenge, so that it would be an inspiration and a reminder to people. This speaks to us today of community, relationships and true joinings in Christ. We are called to demonstrate to those who are close to us what God can and is doing. We are to live our lives in close enough proximity to others that they will observe what we are doing and to be an inspiration to them.

There is emerging on the earth today a true biblical fellowship, a *Koinonia*. This is a work of the Holy Spirit and is essential for the end times. Even in natural families, let them see your life, your example, your witness. It can serve to inspire and motivate others in their walk with Jesus. Paul told Timothy to, *"be an example for the believers in speech, in life, in love, in faith and in purity"* (1 Timothy 4:12).

Repaired The Altar

The second thing we see in this powerful story is Elijah repairing the altar of the Lord which was in ruins. The altar was the place of worship, the place of sacrifice, the place of meeting with God. For us it represents our relationship with the Lord. It should have been a place that the people of God visited regularly, where relationship with their Lord was continually cultivated and nurtured. Instead it had been neglected, forgotten and was in ruins.

Relationships are built on encounters between people. We may call these meetings or conversations. Without regular, intentional meetings or encounters, a relationship will wither and die. We need to visit regularly the "altar" of encounter with God in our lives; to repair the altar if it has broken down and then guard it jealously, nurture it intentionally.

Every believer needs a daily meeting place with God – a regular, designated time and place that has been set aside to meet with their Lord and Saviour. To neglect it is to expose our spiritual life to great danger. It is in these encounters that we receive fresh bread from heaven. Later in the book I will suggest some practically ways in which we can "build" this altar.

Took 12 stones

The 12 stones represented a number of things. It stood for God's Word and His promises to His people regarding all they were to become. It reminded them of His visitation to their forefathers. The stones represented their history. It put their story into context, reminding them that others had gone before and that they were part of a bigger picture – that they must not lose their way, but run their race with perseverance.

"After that generation had been gathered up to their fathers, another generation grew up, who knew neither the Lord, nor the works he had done for Israel. And the Israelites did evil in the eyes of the Lord." (Judges 2:10)

The verse above shows us the danger and potential consequences of forgetting what the Lord has done. It also reminds us why we need to tell our children about all of His great works. We have a spiritual inheritance that needs to be passed safely to our children and our children's children.

The stones were also a symbol of God's goodness. They spoke of His faithfulness. We all need reminders of God's goodness, faithfulness and His enduring love. We must purposefully place "stones" of remembrance in our own lives – things that will remind us and encourage us every time we see them. Maybe you can print out specific scriptures that God has used to speak into your life and place them in strategic positions around your house. They will serve as a reminder of what God has said He will do. Initiate times of telling stories as part of a family devotional time. Record the things God has said or done in your personal journal, so that you can look back and see His hand at work in your life. As Karl Marx once said, "Take away a peoples' heritage and they are easily persuaded." We must not number among those who are easily persuaded away from God's truth. Instead, let us purpose to remember.

Built an altar in the name of the Lord (with these stones)

Elijah was demonstrating to the people that we can build upon God's goodness and His promises because He is faithful and His word is rock solid. We remind ourselves of His past visitations and His commitment to our future in the place of encounter.

"I will remember the deeds of the Lord;
yes, I will remember your miracles of long ago.
I will meditate on all your works
and consider all your mighty deeds.
Your ways, O God, are holy.
What god is so great as our God?
You are the God who performs miracles;
you display your power among the peoples.

With your mighty arm you redeemed your people,

the descendants of Jacob and Joseph." (Psalm 77:11-15)

There is huge value and importance in us cultivating a heart of gratitude and of reminding ourselves daily of God's goodness and His many kindnesses (see Psalm 106:7 & 63:7). It causes our faith to be strengthened and encouraged. It brings to remembrance the previous deliverances and provisions of God. Gratitude puts our immediate circumstances into context and provides strength for the current battle we find ourselves in. I am reminded of an old hymn:

When upon life's billows

You are tempest tossed

When you are discouraged,

Thinking all is lost

Count your many blessings,

Name them one by one

And it will surprise you

What the Lord has done.

Chorus:

Count your blessings,

Name them one by one

Count your blessings,

See what God has done

Count your blessings,

Name them one by one

Count your many blessings,

See what God has done.

Are you ever burdened

With a load of care?

Does the cross seem heavy

You are called to bear?

Count your many blessings,

Ev'ry doubt will fly

And you will be singing

When you look at others

With their lands and gold

Think that Christ has promised

You His wealth untold

Count your many blessings,

Money cannot buy

Your reward in heaven,

Nor your home on high.

So, amid the conflict,

Whether great or small

Do not be discouraged,

God is over all

Count your many blessings,

Angels will attend

Help and comfort give you

To your journey's end.

— *Rev. Johnson Oatman, Jr.*

Dug a large trench

This speaks to us about the importance of creating or clearing space in our lives – space that can be filled with God. Sometimes there is clutter, busyness and a thousand things that have crept into our lives and there is no room for the Lord. Elijah took time and made an effort to dig out the dirt and create space that could contain the water that was to come. He didn't just dig a trench, he dug a "large trench" all around the altar.

We live such hurried lives today that many people only grab a few minutes (if that) to meet with God. But much time must be given if we desire to be fruitful in our relationship with God and be "burning ones". This cannot happen casually. It does not happen for lazy day dreamers and busy bodies. I will speak more about how to practically do this as the book unfolds

Arranged the wood and cut the bull

There are precious things we all need to lay down if we are to surrender to God to the degree which He desires. Some of the things that we cling to may be sinful habits, while others may simply be priorities that have gone awry. Either way, bring them before the Lord and lay them on the altar. Sacrifice is not a dirty word. It is a necessary part of the Christian life.

The Lord has given us many things to enjoy in life and many relationships which we can cherish. But none of these must usurp His place in our lives. Nothing else can become an idol that we worship and adore above Him. We must not even succumb to the subtle trap of allowing the blessings of God to take the place of God Himself.

The relationships the Lord has given us must be kept in their proper place. Abraham knew the joy of receiving the long awaited promise of his son, Isaac, but that same prophetic promise could have become an idol to him. The Lord asked him to sacrifice his son on the altar because nothing can take the place of the Lord in our hearts.

The accumulation of "stuff" has become an epidemic in our culture, to the point where we have so much stuff that we don't know where to put it. Company's now sell storage space for us to keep our stuff because our homes are too small! People are not what they own or what they wear, but this lie is not only in the world, consumerism has also crept into the Church. More than 70 years ago A.W. Tozer spoke about this problem.

"Things were made for man's uses, but they were meant always to be external to the man and subservient to him. In the deep heart of the man was a shrine where none but God was worthy to come. Within him was God; without, a thousand gifts which God had showered upon him ... Our woes began when God was forced out of His central shrine and 'things' were allowed to enter. Within the human heart 'things' have taken over. Men have now by nature no peace within their hearts, for God is crowned there no longer, but there in the moral dusk stubborn and aggressive usurpers fight among themselves for first place on the throne." What do you need to place on the altar?

Poured water on top of it all until it was soaked and the trench full

What Elijah did here seemed absolutely crazy; an illogical thing to do. Wetting the very thing you wanted to set on fire? But the act that was crazy in the natural was the very fuel that made his sacrifice highly flammable. Some say that Elijah did this to prove to the people that there were no human tricks involved, no hidden sleight of hand.

The Bible uses the imagery of both water and fire:

"...to make her holy, cleansing her by the washing with water through the word." (Ephesians 5:26)

"...his word is in my heart like a fire, a fire shut up in my bones. I am weary of holding it in; indeed, I cannot." (Jeremiah 20:9)

For us water represents the cleansing power of the written Word of God, the Bible. This end time army of burning hearts will be constantly immersed in His Word, absorbing its truth. His Word is also like a fire, waiting to burst out. This end time army of burning hearts will have the Word hidden in their hearts and ready in their mouths.

Many miss the power of imbibing the written Word of God. Taken at face value it is easy to underestimate its power. Yet it is one of the most significant disciplines you can give yourself to.

"For the word of God is alive and active. Sharper than any double-edged sword, it penetrates even to dividing soul and spirit, joints and marrow; it judges the thoughts and attitudes of the heart." (Hebrews 4:12)

Jesus said, *"Man does not live by bread alone but by every word that proceeds from the mouth of the father"* (Matthew 4:4)

There is a fascination in the Church today with feelings and things that stir our emotions – and I am all for it! I believe that God created our emotions and that we feel and are, at times, overwhelmed by His love. But we do not live our lives based purely on our feelings. We must build our lives on the foundation of God's Word. When Jesus spoke of the end-times His greatest warning was against error and deception. If you do not know and love the Bible, applying it to your life daily, you will be easily misled or deceived.

Soak in the Bible, overdose on it, read, mediate, store up and confess it. Do not let this book depart from your mouth. I cannot express how strongly I feel about this. I have such a personal sense of urgency to make this one of my highest priorities on a daily basis.

The result, as Elijah did these things, was that when he cried out to the Lord, God answered him with all-consuming heavenly fire. God answers by fire. Do the above and you always get fire, heavenly fire!

IGNITING THE FLAME

- Read again through the story of Elijah in 1 Kings 18 and challenge yourself to make space for a regular place of encounter with God. Do this and He will respond with fire.

I am a disciple of His...

I'm part of the fellowship of the unshamed, I have Holy Spirit power, the die has been cast, I have stepped over the line, the decision has been made, I am a disciple of His. I will not look back, let up, slow down, or back away. My past is redeemed, my present makes sense, my future is secure. I am finished and done with low living, sight walking, small planning, smooth knees, colourless dreams, tamed vision, mundane talking, cheap giving and dwarfed goals. I no longer need pre-eminence, prosperity, position, promotions, applause, its all popularity. I don't need to be right, first, tops, recognised, praised, regarded, or rewarded. I now live by faith, lean on His presence, walk by patience, live by prayer and labour by power. My faith is set. My gait is fast. My goal is heaven. My road is narrow, my way is rough. My companions few. My guide reliable, my mission clear. I cannot be bought, compromised, detoured, lured away, turned back, deluded or delayed. I will not flinch in the face of sacrifice, hesitate in the presence of the adversary, negotiate at the table of the enemy, ponder at the pool of popularity or meander in a maze of mediocrity. I won't give up, shut up, let up, until I have stayed up, stored up, prayed up, paid up, preached up for the cause of Christ. I am a disciple of Jesus Christ. I must go till he comes, give till I drop, preach till all know, and work till He stops me. And, when he comes for His own, He will have no problem recognising me, my banner is clear
- An African Martyr.
'Dear Jesus please make me like this.'

4
Dying To Live

The Company of Burning Ones will have learnt through experience and relationship that the only way to walk in the way of the Spirit, manifesting the power of the Lord, is through death. They will readily and fully embrace this death so that the life of God will flow out through them. Jesus said,

"If anyone would come after me, he must deny himself and take up his cross daily and follow me. For whoever wants to save his life will lose it, but whoever loses his life for me will save it." (Luke 9:23)

True biblical Christianity really begins through death which then leads to life. The problem for many today is that we are trying to access the life and power of God without embracing death. This leads to frustration and weakness in believers who end up living powerless lives, constantly struggling to overcome. It is also the reason we have so many weak, man-made churches which are void of the power of God. The power of the Holy Spirit flows through those who have died and now live to the Spirit.

The words from a greeting card express this well:

All of self, none of God

Less of self, more of God

None of self, all of God

Some have begun to recognise that their lives and ministries are void of New Testament, Holy Spirit power and so have begun speaking about "the power of the Spirit" or about the need for the anointing. But they still manifest little or no power and anointing. Talking about power is not the same as having power. Paul tells us that the Kingdom of God is not a matter of talk, but of power.

A few years ago there was a phrase that kept going through my heart: "The Emperor has no clothes on – he is naked." (the full story is included in the appendix). If you know the children's story the emperor was fooled into thinking he was wearing stunning, beautiful clothes. In reality he was naked. No one was willing to see or speak the truth, except a little boy. Much of the Church is powerless, despite the fact that the Gospel and the Jesus we represent is not powerless. The should not be the case and it need not be. Jesus is all powerful and our representation of Him must be true.

We too must become like little children to enter the kingdom of God and to have the Kingdom flow through our lives.

Right foundations and materials

Like the emperor in the story, some people are too proud or have gone too far to acknowledge their nakedness. There is just too much at stake now for them to admit it. It would mean stopping all they are doing and acknowledging their current reality. It takes humility, honesty and courage to do this – virtues they are unwilling to display, perhaps because they don't possess them or perhaps because they are unwilling to face their fears. Instead, self effort kicks in and they carry on trying to build what only God can build. Many search for principles and methods that will lead to greater power, fruitfulness and increase, but they are ignoring Jesus's command to come to Him and die.

The result is that we can easily end up building our lives, churches and ministries in our own strength, attempting to replicate what others are doing rather than being led by the Holy Spirit. But all that we build during our earthly lifetime will be tested by fire in the light of eternity and everything that is "man made" will be burnt up!

"For no one can lay any foundation other than the one already laid, which is Jesus Christ. If any man builds on this foundation using gold, silver, costly stones, wood, hay or straw, his work will be shown for what it is, because the Day will bring it to light. It will be revealed with fire, and the fire will test the quality of each man's work. If what he has built survives, he will receive his reward. If it is burned up, he will suffer loss; he himself will be saved, but only as one escaping through the flames." (1 Corinthians 3:11-15)

These words of Paul are true and present an extremely serious challenge to us all. We must build our lives and ministries on the foundation of Jesus Christ, because there is no other foundation. Then we must build using the right materials. The perspectives of heaven and earth are vastly different when it comes to judging what is successful or fruitful. They are polar opposites.

The mindsets of too many in the Church are more attuned to the world (the spirit of this age) than they are to the Kingdom of God. What foundation are you building on? Is it stable, secure and trustworthy? These are eternally important questions to answer. If the foundation is anything other than Jesus Christ, then it is extremely unstable to build upon.

A foundation is something at the bedrock upon which you build. People choose all sorts of things as the foundation for their lives, families, churches and ministeries. Some build on their academic achievement, trusting their mind and perhaps even idolising it. Some build on financial stability and the acquisition of wealth, believing that is the most stable, solid foundation for their life and family. These do not realise that they can gain the whole world and yet lose their soul.

There are others who make a human relationship the foundation of their life. It could be a spouse, parents or perhaps children. But these natural relationships will never provide a strong enough base upon which to build our lives. They cannot survive the storms of this life never mind help us in eternity. There is only one true and strong foundation to build upon and that is the person of Jesus Christ. Believing and trusting Him, knowing and applying His words of life secure us to the Rock.

This applies also to churches and ministries. In some churches their particular history and traditions are honoured above Christ. They may very well have a good, godly history that deserves to be celebrated and honoured, but it cannot replace Christ as the foundation.

In some circles the pastor's name or the church's name is given far more prominence and preeminence than Jesus Himself. This has been a problem since the Church began, with the Corinthian church arguing over whether they belonged to Paul or Cephas or Apollos. But it seems to have become more brash and shameless today. This is very dangerous and must be repented of. The Church is the Bride of Christ and must be built upon Him as the Chief Cornerstone. Jesus is the Head of His Church and will not share the place of headship with another. John the baptist made it clear that the Bride belongs to the Bridegroom. As pastors or leaders we must not take the affection that belongs to the Bridegroom and turn it towards ourselves. This is a monstrous perversity and we will have to give account for it to the Bridegroom Himself!

Once the foundation is set correctly we still need to use the right materials for building. The scripture above tells us that we can build using gold, silver, costly stones, wood, hay or straw. Two groupings of materials: the first set is costly and precious and will survive fire. The second set is cheap, common and will be burned up by the fire. Gold, silver and costly stones speak of building according to the mind of Christ, led by the Holy Spirit. It demonstrates a life that is surrendered; a life that exists only to do the Master's bidding.

Like Jesus this person can do nothing of eternal value by themselves, but only does what they see the Father doing. Psalm 133 tells us that, *"unless the Lord builds the house, they that labour do so in vain."* It doesn't say you can't build without Him, just that your work will be in vain, producing no real results. Wood hay and stubble speak of the efforts that come from the mind of man, working in our strength and with our own wisdom. This second work can look good from a distance, but when it is tested by fire it does not survive, because it had no real substance. The foundation was right, but the materials and methods for building were faulty. The Bible says that a person building their life this way will enter heaven by the skin of their teeth, as one escaping the flames.

Are you ready to die?

This brings us back to the theme of this chapter, Dying to Live. It all starts with death. There is no escaping this truth. It is threaded throughout Jesus' teaching and the epistles of Paul. Both Jesus and Paul were examples of dead men walking. They not only taught this, they lived and demonstrated surrendered lives. Jesus said,

"I tell you the truth, unless a kernel of wheat falls to the ground and dies, it remains only a single seed. But if it dies, it produces

many seeds. The man who loves his life will lose it, while the man who hates his life in this world will keep it for eternal life. Whoever serves me must follow me; and where I am, my servant also will be. My Father will honour the one who serves me." (John 12:24-26)

In this passage Jesus is speaking both about His impending death upon the cross, through which many seeds will be produced, and also about the lives of every one of His followers. We see in His obedience to go to the cross an example for ourselves – to take up our cross daily too. A death to our self-life or our soul-life must take place before we can truly become fruitful in the Kingdom of God. It is not spoken about much today, but oh how we need to embrace the biblical pathway to life.

We must embrace a dying to our wants and desires and purpose to live for Him and Him alone. This message is hardly preached from our pulpits today for fear of losing people or upsetting the wealthy in our churches. Our fear of man has surpassed our fear of the Lord. But He is the only One we are to fear. Read these words of the Apostle Paul and then see why he was able to accomplish so much for the Kingdom of God:

"I have been crucified with Christ and I no longer live, but Christ lives in me. The life I live in the body, I live by faith in the Son of God, who loved me and gave himself for me." (Galatians 2:20)

The Father is calling an army of surrendered, burning ones to be fruitful, destroying the works of the enemy wherever they go; men and women who will advance the Kingdom of God by manifesting the life of God in signs, wonders, miracles and salvations. But there is no shortcut, it begins with a surrendered life. The death of our self-life is not to be feared, but willingly embraced. The heavenly Father is all loving and can be trusted with our lives.

Jesus is our ultimate role model for life and ministry. His earthly life was lived as a surrendered life, to do the will of the Father. Every day was lived on purpose, led by the Father through the Holy Spirit in His life. He did nothing of Himself or for Himself, but only what He saw the the Father doing. It is in His embracing of the cross that we see the greatest example.

"Then he said to them, My soul is overwhelmed with sorrow to the point of death. Stay here and keep watch with me. Going a little farther, he fell with his face to the ground and prayed, My Father, if it is possible, may this cup be taken from me. Yet not as I will, but as you will." (Matthew 26:38-39)

Picture the scene: the tension, the impending emotional, physical and then spiritual pain Jesus knew was coming. He is overwhelmed with sorrow to the point of death and He asks His Father, "Is there another way to do this? If so so let's go with the other option, but your will be done. I will do whatever you ask."

It was a surrendering of His own will to the will of the Father. This is the crux of the matter: *are we willing to surrender our will to His will?*

It is a choice, not an emotion. But it is a choice that should not be taken lightly. Take time to consider the outcomes of the choice, talking things through with our Heavenly Father, reflecting upon the Scriptures in this chapter and allowing the Holy Spirit to quicken them to you. I will also add here that we must not fight this, but surrender willingly and delight in doing His will.

This will make it easier and less painful. The reason so many Christians live frustrated, almost tortured lives is because they are trying to keep parts of their life for themselves. They may surrender a little grudgingly and then keep some things back. Then maybe take something back from God and then later surrender a little again. This prolongs the "dying to self" process unnecessarily. Some perpetuate this habit their whole lives.

I don't believe surrender is a one time experience, but there are significant encounters we have with the Lord that mark us and through which a deep work of the Spirit is done. But it also involves a daily surrender to live a life empowered by the Holy Spirit, our will yielding to His will. It demands daily choosing to live under His Lordship, daily preferring others, daily looking for what the Father is doing. That is why Jesus tells us to take up our cross daily and follow Him.

Examples from history

Let me give you some examples from people in history who have inspired me. One of my heroes is Smith Wigglesworth, the uneducated plumber from Bradford, England, who lived during the first half of the last century. He walked in unusual power and communion with the Lord. Miracles were the order of the day and he led many people to the Lord daily, both through public ministry but also through everyday situations. Though he never wrote a book himself many have been written about him since his death. In many of those books the fascination is with the outstanding miracles and supernatural wonders. I too love reading and being stirred by those, but I am also curious as to what enabled him to be the man he was.

I believe every Christian can walk in the same power as he did! Jesus is our example and Smith was simply living the Christ-life. I have read many books about him and here is a quote that helps us to understand what Wigglesworth himself said released the power of God into his life. He was asked during a preaching tour in New Zealand in 1922, what the secret to his power was. Here is his reply:

"In a broken voice, and with tears slowly trickling down his face, he replied: "I am sorry you asked me that question, but I will answer it."

"I am a broken-hearted man. My wife, who meant everything to me, died eleven years ago (in 1913). After the funeral, I went back and lay on her grave. I wanted to die there. But God spoke to me and told me to rise up and come away. I told him if he would give me a double portion of the Spirit – my wife's and my own – I would go and preach the Gospel. God was gracious to me and answered my request. But I sail the high seas alone. I am a lonely man, and many a time all I can do is to weep and weep."

Here was a secret indeed.

"The sacrifices of God are a broken spirit a broken and contrite heart, O God, thou wilt not despise." (Psalm 51:17)

Here is one more simple but profound quote from one of Wigglesworth's sermons:

"Before God could bring me to this place He has broken me a thousand times."

Another one of my inspirations is George Muller, the German missionary who moved to England in 1829 and began a ministry that spanned almost 70 years. He built 5 large orphanages, was the pastor of a 1200 member church, ran a publishing house and after the age of 70 did three world preaching tours! Among the many things he is known for is the miraculous way he prayed in resources to build his children's homes and to run his publishing house. He took no set salary from the church or the homes; he never made any need he had public or took an offering.

And yet he prayed in 1.5 million pounds during his lifetime! In today's money that would be more than 30 million! He lived by the conviction that he need only tell his Heavenly Father of his need and all would be well. The stories of provision are breathtaking and nothing short of miraculous. He was known best as a man who knew how to get prayers answered. In a ministers meeting nearer the end of his life he was asked how he managed to see such miraculous fruitfulness in his life. Here is his answer:

"There was a day when I died;

died to self, my opinions, preferences, tastes and will;

died to the world, its approval or censure;

died to the approval or blame even of my brethren or friends;

and since then I have studied only

to show myself approved unto God."

My final example is from the life of Rees Howell who lived 100 years ago and was a powerful intercessor for the Lord. He was a man of deep prayer and quick obedience to the Lord. The following is taken from Norman Grubb's book, *The Intercessor*.

"The meeting with the Holy Ghost was just as real to Rees Howells as his meeting with the Saviour those years before. 'I saw Him as a Person apart from flesh and blood, and He said to me, "As the Saviour had a body, so I dwell in the cleansed temple of the believer. I am a Person. I am God, and I am come to ask you to give your body to Me that I may work through it. I need a body for My temple (1 Cor. 6:19), but it must belong to Me without reserve, for two persons with different wills can never live in the same body. Will you give Me yours? (Rom. 12:1). But if I come in, I come as God, and you must go out (Col. 3:2, 3). I shall not mix Myself with your self."

'He made it very plain that He would never share my life. I saw the honour He gave me in offering to indwell me, but there were many things very dear to me, and I knew He wouldn't keep one of them. The change He would make was very clear. It meant every bit of my fallen nature was to go to the cross, and

He would bring in His own life and His own nature.'

It was unconditional surrender. From the meeting Rees went out into a field, where he cried his heart out, because, as he said, 'I had received a sentence of death, as really as a prisoner in the dock. I had lived in my body for twenty-six years, and could I easily give it up? Who could give his life up to another person in an hour? Why does a man struggle when death comes, if it is easy to die? I knew that the only place fit for the old nature was on the cross. Paul makes that very plain in Romans 6. But once this is done in reality, it is done for ever. I could not run into this. I intended to do it, but oh, the cost! I wept for days. I lost seven pounds in weight, just because I saw what He was offering me. How I wished I had never seen it! One thing He reminded me of was that He had only come to take what I had already promised the Saviour, not in part, but the whole. Since He died for me, I had died in Him, and I knew that the new life was His and not mine. That had been clear in my mind for three years; so He had only come to take what was His own: and I saw that only the Holy Ghost in me could live like the Saviour. Everything He told me appealed to me; it was only a question of the loss there would be in doing it. I didn't give my answer in a moment, and He didn't want me to.'

It took five days to make the decision, days which were spent alone with God. 'Like Isaiah, I saw the holiness of God,' he said, 'and seeing Him, I saw my own corrupt nature. It wasn't sins that I saw, but nature touched by the Fall. I was corrupt to the core. I knew I had to be cleansed; I saw there was as much difference between the Holy Ghost and myself as between light and darkness.'

'Nothing is more real to me than the process I went through for that whole week,' he continued. 'The Holy Spirit went on dealing with me, exposing the root of my nature which was self, and you can only get out of a thing what is in its root. Sin was cancelled, and it wasn't sin He was dealing with; it was self -- that thing which came from the Fall. He was not going to take any superficial surrender. He put His finger on each part of my self-life, and I had to decide in cold blood. He could never take a thing away until I gave my consent. Then the moment I gave it, some purging took place (Isaiah 6:5-7), and I could never touch that thing again. It was not saying I was purged and the thing still having a hold on me: no, it was a breaking, and the Holy Ghost taking control. Day by day the dealing went on. He was coming in as God, and I had lived as man, and "what is permissible to an ordinary man," He told me, "will not be permissible to you."''

I could give many more examples, but I think enough has been said for now. I encourage you to put the book down for a while and have sometime reflecting and talking to the Lord about what He is requiring of you. His grace and mercy are freely offered to you.

IGNITING THE FLAME

- If you are really serious about becoming one of God's Burning

Ones there is a cost involved. It demands that we lay down our life to the One who can cause us to truly live. There can be no life without death.

- Take time to talk to God about what this means. This can be no half-hearted surrender. We can't make the choice and then try to take it back from the Lord. Rees Howells considered the severity of his commitment to God for a week, weighing up the cost of surrender. Take time to do the same yourself.

We have instructed the Church in nearly everything but becoming disciples of Jesus Christ. We have filled the people with doctrine instead of deity; we have given them manuals instead of Emmanuel. Our quest is to be like Jesus, not men; we want the Kingdom of God, not typical Western Christianity.

– Francis Frangipane

5
One Magnificent Obsession

One of the great hallmarks of this Company of Burning Hearts will be their absolute love for and devotion to Jesus Christ. This devotion to Christ will eclipse all other loves in their lives. Their hearts will be on fire for Him, for His presence and to live only to please Him. It will be evident that Christ is living in them by the power of the Holy Spirit because they will manifest Him through their lives. They will be able to say, like the Apostle John, *"That which we have seen with our eyes, we have looked at and our hands have touched..."* They are people who don't just know about Jesus, but they *know* Him, intimately.

God is awakening people so that their relationship with Him is not reduced to a formula or a prayer, but is a living, dynamic, reality with substance. Here are Jesus' very own words, explaining what eternal life or salvation is. There is no better definition than the one He gives to us:

"Now this is eternal life: that they may know you, the only true God, and Jesus Christ whom you have sent." (John 17:3)

Our walk with God was always meant to be relational, but over time it has been hijacked by the traditions of men and dry, man-made theology. Salvation is not primarily about getting us to heaven, it is about getting us to the heavenly Father. Yes, we get to go to heaven, but Jesus came to reconcile a broken relationship between man and God, so that God may dwell in humans again through the work of Jesus on the cross and by the power of the Holy Spirit.

Jesus said, *"I am the way, the truth and the life, no one comes to the Father but by me"* (John 14:6). So now through Christ Jesus, God lives in us and heaven comes to earth. We become gateways for the Kingdom of God upon the earth. The goal was never just to get to us heaven, but to release heaven's dominion on the earth through redeemed humans. This is the gospel and the foundation will always remain Jesus – because without Christ and faith in His finished work, their is no salvation.

Many preach the "gospel" without preaching Jesus, but this cannot lead to new birth. The power lies in Christ's work at the cross. Thats why the Apostle Paul said,

"When I came to you, brothers, I did not come with eloquence or superior wisdom as I proclaimed to you the testimony about God. For I resolved to know nothing while I was with you except Jesus Christ and him crucified." (1 Corinthians 2:1-2)

To pray a quick prayer in order to gain a "free pass" to heaven is not the good news of the New Testament. John Piper says,

"People who would be happy in heaven if Christ were not there will not be there. The gospel is not a way to get people into heaven; it is a way to get people to God. It's a way of overcoming every obstacle to everlasting joy in God. If we don't want God above all things, we have not been converted by the gospel." Jesus has been pushed to the sidelines and, in many places, is the forgotten man of the gospel. Some still mention or sing His name, but the reality of His person is forgotten and ignored. Many believers are now captivated and fascinated by His "blessings" or even by "working for Him" and some by the temporal, fleeting things of this world. Perhaps the words of Jesus two thousand years ago are more poignant now than even in His time.

"'These people honour me with their lips,
but their hearts are far from me.
They worship me in vain;
their teachings are but rules taught by men."
(Matthew 15:8-9)

This is nothing new, it happened in Jesus day and throughout Church history, but it must not be this way. Jesus Christ is the only foundation we can build our lives, families and churches upon. Paul told the church at Corinth, *"For no one can lay any foundation other than the one already laid, which is Jesus Christ"* (1 Corinthians 3:11). He is King and He is coming back to take His rightful place in our hearts and also in His Church. He will not share His glory with another.

Some want to have Jesus but also keep hold of other things, material things. In many parts of the Church people are devoted to their buildings, brands (things) and even pet doctrines. I love the local church and have the great privilege of leading a local church, but we must not love the Body and forget the Head or be focused on the Bride and pay little or no attention to the Bridegroom. All kinds of strange and weird stuff has polluted and distracted the preaching of the gospel. In fact, some think they are preaching the gospel but Jesus and His work on the cross are never mentioned! Altar calls are given without an explanation of the work of Jesus on the cross, paying the price for our sins.

An unpreached gospel is no gospel at all! Giving people an emotional worship experience or a moving, stirring talk is not the gospel. I actually think many believers and even preachers today don't really understand the good news of Jesus. He took human form (the incarnation) and became obedient to death as our sacrifice and in our place, so that we may be reconciled to the Father. This is the wonderful gospel and the only sure foundation to build upon. The old hymn writer from 1834 put it so beautifully:

My hope is built on nothing less
Than Jesus' blood and righteousness.
I dare not trust the sweetest frame,
But wholly trust in Jesus' Name.

Refrain
On Christ the solid Rock I stand,
All other ground is sinking sand;
All other ground is sinking sand.

When darkness seems to hide His face,
I rest on His unchanging grace.
In every high and stormy gale,
My anchor holds within the veil.

His oath, His covenant, His blood,
Support me in the whelming flood.
When all around my soul gives way,
He then is all my Hope and Stay.

When He shall come with trumpet sound,
Oh may I then in Him be found.
Dressed in His righteousness alone,
Faultless to stand before the throne.
– *Edward Mote*

Jesus – The head and the heart

"He is before all things, and in him all things hold together. he is the head of the body, the Church; he is the beginning and the firstborn from among the dead, so that in everything he might have the supremacy." (Colossians 1:17-18)

I want to bring your attention to two things from the passage above. Jesus is the Head of His Body, meaning He should be above all things and have supremacy in everything.

Secondly, *"in him all things hold together"*, means that He should be at the heart of everything, giving life to and holding it all together.

His Headship, or we could call it his Lordship, should be absolute in our lives, families, ministries and churches. This really is not an option for believers, but a requirement and expectation from Jesus's own teaching. Let's look at Jesus' own words:

"Not everyone who says to me, 'Lord, Lord,' will enter the kingdom of heaven, but only he who does the will of my Father

who is in heaven." (Matthew 7:21)

Once we have come into relationship with the Father through the Son by the power of the Holy Spirit, the adventure begins. It requires us to become His disciple, learning from the Master and submitting to Him in all areas of our life. This end-time Company of Burning Ones will not hold back anything from their Lord and Saviour. It is our responsibility to learn His ways, His teachings given to us in the Bible; and not only learning them, but obeying them and conforming our lives to His life and teaching. There is a tremendous secret in quick and full obedience. The wonderful truth is that He not only shows us what to do, but enables and empowers us to do it. In our own strength we are limited and cannot achieve the commands of the Bible, but it is not a matter of our efforts. The Holy Spirit Himself becomes our helper.

I am convinced that if people seriously considered the issue of the supremacy of Christ in their lives and then submitted to Him, it would lead to dynamic fruitfulness and a release of God's power in and through them. Many live mediocre lives and go through unnecessary battles and trials simply because they hold onto areas of their lives and will not surrender them to the Lordship of Jesus. Let me make it really clear: Jesus' Lordship must touch our relationships, money, ambitions, careers, leisure time and everything else. He is either Lord of all or not Lord at all.

Heart

"So then, just as you received Christ Jesus as Lord, continue to live in him, rooted and built up in him, strengthened in the faith as you were taught, and overflowing with thankfulness." (Colossians 2:6-7)

Not only is Jesus the Head, He is also the heart. We find our strength and stamina coming from the grace and power He supplies. The scripture above is so powerful – we can live "in Christ" and are rooted into Him, receiving strength minute by minute, hour by hour and day by day. You can know this and you should know this divine help that is available to every child of God. Many have never experienced this dynamic of divine life flowing through their very bodies and minds. Yet Paul urges us that this is the way all believers can and should live. It is a choice to live this way, that is why we are told to do so.

Jesus must also be the centre of our lives. He must be the centre of my marriage, my family and all my planning. He must be the very core of ministry work and church building. If our lives, marriages, parenting and work are all rooted in Him, what wonderful and lasting fruit will be born and what amazing, divine life and energy will flow through every area of our lives! The Christian life is not a buffet meal from which you can pick and choose as you like, it is an all-consuming relationship with the Creator of the universe, made possible by His own Son's death.

First love

"I know your deeds, your hard work and your perseverance. I know that you cannot tolerate wicked men, that you have tested those who claim to be apostles but are not, and have found them false. You have persevered and have endured hardships for my name, and have not grown weary. Yet I hold this against you: You have forsaken your first love. Remember the height from which you have fallen! Repent and do the things you did at first." (Revelation 2:2-5)

All we have spoken about so far in this chapter comes back to being rooted in love for Jesus and knowing His lavish, amazing love for us. The Christian Gospel is really the most amazing love story ever told. Love is at the core of it. God Himself is the embodiment of love. With that in mind let's explore what Jesus has to say to us about our love for Him. Here is a list of the good things that the church at Ephesus were commended for:

- Hard work
- Perseverance
- Not tolerating wicked men
- Testing false apostles
- Persevering and enduring hardship in the name of Jesus
- Not growing weary

This is a wonderful list of things the church was doing well. Perhaps if we went to a church like this we would feel proud to belong there. But not Jesus. He is about to rebuke them for missing something that was most important. *"Yet I hold this against you: You have forsaken your first love."* They had forsaken their love for God. Yes, they were busy working hard and even endured hardships, persevering through them without becoming weary. But they had forsaken, deserted, abandoned their love for Jesus. Oh, what a tragedy, what a dangerous and costly thing to do and yet many still do this today. We get busy working for the Lord and can easily forget that the Lord is more concerned about the state of our hearts towards Him.

Jesus gives them and us a remedy to such a problem. *"Remember the height from which you have fallen! Repent and do the things you did at first."* Many people need to get back to ground zero, thinking of the first days in which they followed

Christ, and realise how far they have gone astray in their faith. They need to reconnect with their passion for Jesus. Repentance is a complete change of mind, our thinking reversed – no longer putting the work of the Lord before the Lord of the work. It is a decision we make – not rooted in an emotional response, but in a firm commitment to remedy that which has gone wrong.

Then Jesus instructs the church to do the things they did at first. Can you remember the things you did at first, before you got engrossed in the "work"? "First Love" speaks of two things here: the love you had at the beginning of your conversion, but also the fact that Jesus must be your First Love, above all other loves.

Jesus warned this church that they if they did not heed His warning and change, He would come and remove their lampstand. The lampstand represented the church itself. Jesus felt so strongly about this that He would remove the church from its place! God is not a task master, looking for us to work harder and perform ever more for His kingdom. He is a lover looking for our hearts to filled with His love and for us to be growing relationally in our knowledge of Him, thereby bringing Him glory.

Yes, I believe in working hard, but we can't put the cart before the horse. Our lives must flow in the correct way, the Kingdom way – as a dynamic love relationship, expressed through the Lordship of the King in our lives, in our work, in our church, in our families.

"But seek first his kingdom and his righteousness, and all these things will be given to you as well." (Matthew 6:33)

I want to finish this chapter with a quote from Pastor John

Piper, from his book *Sex and the Supremacy of Christ*, that has so enriched my thinking about Jesus.

"Knowing the supremacy of Christ enlarges the soul so that the world and its little thrills become as small as they really are. Little souls make little lusts have great power. The soul, as it were, expands to encompass the magnitude of its treasure. The human soul was made to see and savour the supremacy of Christ. Nothing else is big enough to enlarge the soul as God intended and make little lusts lose their power.

Vast starry skies seen from a mountain in Utah and four layers of moving clouds on a seemingly endless plain in Montana, and standing on the edge of a mile-deep drop in the Grand Canyon can all have a wonderfully supplementary role in enlarging the soul with beauty. But nothing can take the place of the supremacy of Christ. As Jonathan Edwards said, if you embrace all creation with goodwill, but not Christ, you are infinitely parochial. Our hearts were made to be enlarged by Christ, and all creation cannot replace his supremacy.

My conviction is that one of the main reasons the world and the church are awash in lust and pornography is that our lives are intellectually and emotionally disconnected from infinite, soul-staggering grandeur for which we were made. Inside and outside the church western culture is drowning in a sea of triviality, pettiness, banality, and silliness. Television is trivial. Radio is trivial. Conversation is trivial. Education is trivial. Christian books are trivial. Worship styles are trivial. It is inevitable that the human heart, which was made to be staggered with the supremacy of Christ, but instead is drowning in a sea of banal entertainment, will reach for the best natural buzz that life can give: sex. Therefore, the deepest cure to our pitiful addictions is not any mental strategies. The deepest cure is to be intellectually and emotionally and relationally staggered by the infinite, everlasting, unchanging supremacy of Christ in all things. This is what it means to know him. Christ has purchased this gift for us at the cost of his life."

IGNITING THE FLAME

- One of the great lessons we can draw from Jesus' letters to the churches in Revelation is that we can think our spiritual lives are going well, whilst at the same time having fallen into a formulaic existence without realising it. Instead we are called to a dynamic, living, moving relationship with God. Meditate on the truth that God is not a task master who wants us to perform for Him. He is a Lover who wants us to be immersed in the joy of knowing Him deeply.

- Spend some time reflecting on your life at the time when you came to Christ. Are there things you once did that you need to reconnect with? Allow God to rekindle your First Love.

Ah, God, what a new nearness this brings for
Thee and me, to realise that Thou alone canst
understand me, for Thou alone knowest all!
Thou art no longer a stranger, God!
Thou art the only being in the universe who is
not partly a stranger! Thou art all the way inside
with me here ... I mean to struggle tonight and
tomorrow as never before, not once to dismiss
Thee. For when I lose Thee for an hour I lose.
The thing Thou wouldst do can only be done when
Thou hast full sway all the time. Last Monday was
the most completely successful day of my life to
date, so far as giving my day in complete and
continuous surrender to God is concerned...
I remember how as I looked at people with a love
God gave, they looked back and acted as though
they wanted to go with me. I felt then that for a
day I saw a little of that marvellous pull that Jesus
had as He walked along the road day after day
'God-intoxicated' and radiant with the endless
communion of His soul with God!
                                    - Frank Luabach

6
Just Like Jesus

Not only are we to be in a dynamic love relationship with Jesus, but we are being changed through that relationship to become just like Him. It is extremely exciting that God doesn't leave us as He found us, but helps us to change to become like His Son, Jesus. This is the beautiful adventure that we are on. There is nothing more exciting than a transformed life. Paul put it this way:

"For those God foreknew he also predestined to be conformed to the likeness of his Son, that he might be the firstborn among many brothers." (Romans 8:29)

God has destined us to be conformed to the likeness of Jesus. He calls Him the "firstborn among many" meaning that there will be many more children, all of them carrying the same family likeness. Our journey doesn't end with salvation. It has only just begun. Now the very one who saved us desires to live in and through us. The reason this is exciting is that it is through this process of transformation that God can manifest

His power in a greater way through us. I heard a preacher say that, "Christlikeness is the currency of heaven." In other words, the more like Him we look, the greater our buying power.

The devil is not afraid of you, but he is afraid of Christ in you. It is Christ in you the hope of glory (Colossians 1:27). The more like Jesus you become, the more dangerous you are to the domain of darkness. The more like Jesus you become, the greater the fruitfulness will occur in your life.

Let me give you a couple more scriptures that confirm that this is the Lord's will for your life. Please read these carefully and don't skip over the them. The Word of God is extremely powerful.

*"My dear children, for whom I am again in the pains of childbirth **until Christ is formed in you**."* (Galatians 4:19)

This shows Paul's deep desire and passion for the church at Galatia to look like and behave like Christ. He says he is experiencing similar pains as a mother about to give birth to a child as he works and prays for Christ to be formed in them. You get the impression that his praying for them and writing to them is born out of an intense longing for them to become just like Jesus.

"Whoever claims to live in him must walk as Jesus did." (1 John 2:6)

Like Paul, the Apostle John carries the same message, both in his first epistle and in his gospel. If you say you are in God then prove it by walking like Jesus. That is strong talk from him. It is not an option but a command: "must walk" as Jesus did.

Today's Church has believed a lie that God's primary purpose is to bless them or make their life easier. This is not true. God is far more concerned about forming the likeness of His Son in you than giving you a comfortable life. There may be some who think their "work for God" excuses them from being like Jesus. Francis Frangipane brings great clarity to that deception.

"We define ourselves by what we do for God rather than what we become to Him. What pleases the Father most is not what proceeds from our hands but what rises from our hearts. He is seeking the revelation of His Son in us."

Ephesians 4 is an important chapter regarding our journey to becoming like Christ. I encourage you to read and meditate on the first sixteen verses. Let me just focus on verses 12-16:

"...to prepare God's people for works of service, so that the body of Christ may be built up until we all reach unity in the faith and in the knowledge of the Son of God and become mature, attaining to the whole measure of the fullness of Christ."

Paul tell us that we have been given leaders by God and they prepare us for works of ministry so that we can be built up until we reach unity in the faith and in the knowledge of Christ. Then we are becoming mature, attaining to the whole measure of the fullness of Christ. Do you see that? The aim isn't working for God, but to become like Christ: leaders given, work done, growing in maturity and finally becoming like Christ.

Like Jesus in character and power

"I tell you the truth, anyone who has faith in me will do what I have been doing. He will do even greater things than these, because I am going to the Father." (John 14:12)

"I have set you an example that you should do as I have done for you." (John 13:15)

There is no greater testimony than Jesus' very own words and here we have two vital scriptures – though we could have picked far more. They show us two vital aspects of our journey to Christlikeness – power and character. The first scripture tells us that we need to imitate Jesus by moving in God's power like He did. The second scripture shows how we must imitate Jesus' in character. These are not optional extras we can bolt onto our faith as we see fit. You and I are called to be like Jesus in every area of our lives.

Some try to hide behind the gifts of the Spirit and think that because they operate in the gifts they are excused from having their character shaped by God. Others think that because they have the fruit of the Spirit developing, affecting their character, they are somehow excused from manifesting His power. We need both to get the job done. The good news is that both are available and the Burning Ones for whom this book is written will be strong in both these areas.

Let me illustrate a few ways in which this process of change takes place in our lives.

The Holy Spirit

"And I will ask the Father, and he will give you another Counselor to be with you forever – the Spirit of truth. The world cannot accept him, because it neither sees him nor knows him. But you know him, for he lives with you and will be in you. I will not leave you as orphans; I will come to you." (John 14:16-18)

The Holy Spirit is a key person in this whole process. He is the one who forms the likeness of Christ in us. He is both the giver of the gifts (1 Corinthians 12:7-11) and the one who forms the fruit in our lives (Galatians 5:22-25). In our own efforts this would be completely impossible. It is a work of God within our lives. But we must work with the Holy Spirit for this to happen, yielding our will to Him and choosing His way. It is important to understand that we are not trying to mimic or copy Christ. Rather it is the very life of Christ being expressed through us – Christ is in us. It is His nature that manifests through our flesh and blood. Paul knew the working of that divine life in and through him.

"To this end I labour, struggling with all his energy, which so powerfully works in me." (Colossians 1:29)

The Holy Spirit will lead us into all truth. He is the one who quickens the Bible to us, causing it to come alive and give us revelation. He will convict us when we are making wrong choices or behaving in ways that are contrary to our Christ-nature. Not only does He convict, but He also provides the power for us to change, to resist sin and submit to the way of the Lord. It is so wonderful that the Lord not only tells us how to live, but through the Holy Spirit provides the very power we need to do it. We really can do all things through Christ who strengthens us (Philippians 4:13).

By beholding Jesus

"But whenever anyone turns to the Lord, the veil is taken away. Now the Lord is the Spirit, and where the Spirit of the Lord is, there is freedom. And we, who with unveiled faces all reflect the Lord's glory, are being transformed into his likeness with ever-increasing glory, which comes from the Lord, who is the Spirit." (2 Corinthians 3:16-18)

We are also changed by looking to Jesus. Look at the progression in this scripture. First there is a turning towards the Lord to look upon Him. Then we begin to reflect the very glory we are gazing upon. In the simple act of beholding Him in His Word or His presence, a great work is accomplished within us.

My friend Bob Sorge, in his book *Secrets of the Secret Place*, says it so well:

"When you're in His presence for extended periods, the molecular composition of your soul gets restructured. You start to think differently, and you don't even know why. You start to have different passions and interests, and you don't even know why. God is changing you on the inside in ways you can't cognitively analyse. All you know is, sinful affections that once pulled at your soul no longer have their former power over you. The secret is simply this: large chunks of time in God's presence

– loving Him and imbibing His word."

I have said for years that whatever you look at you become like. Many Christians are depressed, confused and anxious because of the time they spend watching the entertainment of this world. It dulls their senses. They absorb the confusion, violence and depression into themselves and then wonder what happened. Change what you are looking at. Look to Christ, both in His Word and in His manifest presence. These are both readily available for you, they just take a little more engagement and effort than turning the TV on.

"Finally, brothers, whatever is true, whatever is noble, whatever is right, whatever is pure, whatever is lovely, whatever is admirable – if anything is excellent or praiseworthy – think about such things." (Philippians 4:8)

God uses situations and people

The Bible tells me that *"all things work together for the good of those who love him, who have been called according to his purpose"* (Romans 8:28). The very next verse speaks about being conformed to the image of Christ. If all things work for my good to produce Christ in me, then I am convinced that God uses people and situations to change me. There is no accident or chance in the circumstances of my life or the people I encounter. Some of these may be difficult and others a blessing, but all can work for my good.

You may be wanting deliverance from the trial you are going

through and I am sure it will come, but the main point is not deliverance. Ask the questions, "Lord what can I learn through this problem? What are you wanting to change in me? How would Jesus respond if He were here?" Because the truth is, He is with you and wants to manifest through you.

I have heard it said and have said it myself: "Never waste a good trial." If embraced with the right attitude and perspective, trials can help show us what is in our hearts and then also reveal the grace of God through us, if we respond rightly. These can be powerful transforming moments that mark us and take us to a new level in our walk with Jesus.

To waste a trial would be to blame, accuse, become bitter and look for a quick exit without discerning our own heart and the voice of the Lord. Smith Wigglesworth put it beautifully:

"Every trial is a blessing. There have been times when I have been pressed through circumstances and it seemed as if a dozen road engines were going over me, but I have found that the hardest things are just lifting places into the grace of God. We have such a lovely Jesus. He always proves Himself to be such a mighty Deliverer. He never fails to plan the best things for us."

I pray that this would be your response and become your experience. When pressure is applied to a wet sponge, water comes out. When pressure is applied to you, what comes out? Christ should ooze out of every Christian. Trials and difficult or awkward people are opportunities to deepen our trust in God. They are an invitation to shine like Jesus. Don't waste a good trial.

The Father loves His Son

Our heavenly Father loves His Son. He shouted His love from heaven at Jesus' baptism. I believe that the Father still loves seeing His Son manifest through flesh and blood!

Through your body and my body, we have the phenomenal opportunity of bringing pleasure to the Father through manifesting Jesus. Francis Frangipane says, "When we awaken the pleasure of God, the power of God will soon follow." This truly is the pathway to Kingdom power.

Transformation doesn't happen instantly but takes time. The New Testament word for this is *metamorphoo* – to change into another form, to transform, to transfigure. It is the root of our word "metamorphosis" which describes what happens when a caterpillar becomes a butterfly or a tadpole becomes a frog. There is a *complete* change. This is what Paul describes in 2 Corinthians 3:18. But it is a process that takes time. We change little by little. I say this to encourage you not to get discouraged on your journey. Stay in the cocoon while the Holy Spirit brings the change within you. The Burning Ones who are arising on the earth will be powerful, unstoppable, known in heaven and hell. It is this characteristic of Christlikeness that will make them so contagious and dangerous. Jesus said in John 14:30, *"The prince of this world is coming. He has no hold on me."* The same verse in the Amplified version reads:

"I will not talk with you much more, for the prince (evil genius, ruler) of the world is coming. And he has no claim on Me. He has

nothing in common with Me; there is nothing in Me that belongs to him, and he has no power over Me." (John 14:30 AMP)

This is what we desire to be like: people over whom the enemy has no hold, no button he can push. People who cannot be irritated into a place of agitation or sin by others. People for whom no lust or sin can cause us to crumble and succumb. People who have no desire to be drawn out of the Father's rest and presence. Is this possible? Yes, because the greater One lives inside of you and will empower you to do it. Embrace this pathway with all your heart and the glorious light you emanate in the Spirit will become so radiant! This is how families, towns and cities will be transformed – by thousands upon thousands of Christlike believers radiating light into darkness and seeing the darkness flee.

IGNITING THE FLAME

- Pray this prayer from modern mystic Frank Laubach, who lived his life pursuing the cause of Christlikeness. Mediate on the words:

  "Lord, let me open my soul to you. Let me open my life to you. I don't want to live a mere fantasy. I want to be like Jesus. I lay my life at your disposal. I know that what Jesus taught is true and is possible. I can be like Him. I want to spend the rest of my life in eternity doing just that. Amen."

To have found God and still to pursue
    Him is the soul's paradox of love,
    scorned indeed by the too-easily-
    satisfied religionist, but justified in
    happy experience by the children of the
    burning heart. St. Bernard stated
    this holy paradox in a musical quatrain
    that will be instantly understood by every
                    worshipping soul:
    We taste Thee? O Thou Living Bread,
        And long to feast upon Thee still:
        We drink of Thee, the Fountainhead
        And thirst our souls from Thee to fill.
                        - AW Tozer

7
Fuelling The Fire

It's a wonderful, life-transforming experience to be awakened by an encounter with the Lord and to feel His presence burning within you. It's in those special moments we know the intimate reality of His love, His insurmountable hope fills our hearts and we have an audacious faith for the future. Biblical faith, hope and love are the reality we are created to live in and from. But this only comes through proximity to the Lord Himself.

Many experience this only for a day, a week or from time to time at special events or conferences. We begin to believe that it is normal to live "in and out" of this experience – that such things are special moments, only to be enjoyed a few times during our earthly life. But this is not the case. We are created to live continually in that place of overcoming faith and buoyant hope, expressing itself through lavish love. This is how George Muller described it in his New Year's address of 1857 :

"Above all things, see to it that your souls are happy in the Lord. Other things may press upon you; the Lord's work even may have urgent claims upon your attention; but I deliberately repeat, it is of supreme and paramount importance that you should seek, above all other things, to have your souls truly happy in God Himself. Day by day seek to make this the most important business of your life. This has been my firm and settled conviction for the last five-and thirty years. For the first four years after my conversion I knew not its vast importance; but now, after much experience, I specially commend this point to the notice of my younger brethren and sisters in Christ. The secret of all true effectual service is, joy in God, and having (experiential) acquaintance and fellowship with God Himself."

Any relationship or "fire", if it is left unattended, will eventually wane and go cold. I have had to contend for this in my own walk with Jesus. I have also counselled others, who told me what they used to be like, how high their passion used to be, or have described to me the intensity of their love for Jesus in the past. An initial encounter with God isn't enough to fuel an individual for the rest of their lives. This is a relationship and like any natural relationship it needs to be intentionally nurtured and cultivated.

Many ministers of the Lord do not live in this place of "continual burning". They do not believe it is possible, perhaps because their experience of life and ministry has been tough and their initial passion has been tempered by life's experiences and disappointments. The problem is, we have created an "experiential" theology rather than a biblical one. Jesus is our ultimate example and role model. If we study His life we see that His faith, love and hope never waned. He lived in relational encounter with His Father each and every day. Consider these words:

"I tell you the truth, the Son can do nothing by himself; he can do only what he sees his Father doing, because whatever the Father does the Son also does." (John 5:19)

"Zeal for thy house consumes me." (Psalm 69:9)

Jesus' life was marked by this passion and obedience which came from living in intimate and intense relationship with His Father. I am not saying that this is an easy place to get to or that it is without persecution or trouble. Jesus had plenty of that. He was rejected almost daily, misunderstood by the religious leaders of His day (who even conspired to kill him) and many disciples turned away from Him (John 6:66). But through it all Jesus was living close to His Father and not distracted from His call and purpose. I believe that not only can we live in that place of encounter, but God's desire and design is that our relationship with Him grows and deepens over time. The way that happens is for us to meet with our Heavenly Father every day. Again Jesus is our example and His life and ministry are conspicuously marked by this habit.

"Very early in the morning, while it was still dark, Jesus got up, left the house and went off to a solitary place, where he prayed." (Mark 1:35)

"After he had dismissed them, he went up on a mountainside by himself to pray." (Matthew 14:23)

"Each day Jesus was teaching at the temple, and each evening he went out to spend the night on the hill called the Mount of Olives." (Luke 21:37)

Daily relational encounter

In the rest of this chapter I want to us to explore together how we can have a *daily relational encounter* with our Heavenly Father. I want to make this really practical and show you ways to fuel your fire and grow in your relationship with the Father. Please bear in mind that having a daily relational time is not the goal. Growing in depth and intimacy in the relationship is the goal. And even this is only the starting point that can lead us to a place where we learn to abide in Him.

I call it a daily relational encounter because so many Christians have "quiet times" in which they don't actually *meet* with their Heavenly Father. It is very easy to go through a ritual of reading and even praying without engaging relationally with the one about whom we read and to whom we pray. Religious duty will never satisfy the deep longing of the human heart. In fact, thousands of people fulfil religious duty while their hearts are harbouring sin and unforgiveness. Jesus said this about the religious leaders of His day: *"These people honour me with their lips but their hearts are from me"* (Matthew 15:8)

Paul warned Timothy that there would be people who have a "form of godliness but deny it's power". We need God's power to overcome sin, so it no longer has a hold on us; power to forgive and respond like Christ; power to heal the sick and destroy the works of the evil one. This power only comes from intimacy. Too many have settled for the form without the power. In every meeting we have with God, we are changed. He never leaves us the same after any encounter. Growing up I was led to believe that most of my quiet times would be dry and boring, but that that was okay and that I should do them anyway. I have since learnt that if I approach the Father relationally, with faith, then every encounter can be a life-transforming one.

I encourage you to make this kind of meeting with God a priority in your life. Make it a daily occurrence and, as much as is possible, go to the same place. It should be a quiet place where you will not be disturbed. Turn your phone or other gadgets off or onto silent. Prepare your heart for a meeting with the Lover of your soul. God will never disappoint an earnest and diligent seeker (Hebrews 11:6). He will be waiting for you. He desires to both listen and speak to you.

Now I want to give you five simple ingredients to a fruitful daily meeting with the Lord.

1. Go with a relational attitude

A.W. Tozer said, "We have almost forgotten that God is a Person and, as such, can be cultivated as any person can. It is inherent in personality to be able to know other personalities, but full knowledge of one personality by another cannot be achieved in one encounter. It is only after long and loving mental intercourse that the full possibilities of both can be explored."

This ingredient is more about our attitude and expectation than something we do. It requires the individual to be expectant to meet with God. We anticipate that there will be two-way communication; both listening and speaking are to take place. I often start my time with the Lord by simply telling Him,

"Good morning Lord. I am here, I desire to meet with you. Thank you that you love me and you also want to be with me and speak to me. Open my eyes, help to see, open my ears and help me to hear. Lord give me a soft and understanding heart. May I know the nearness of your presence today. I live only for your glory and worship you this morning..."

We must fight the tendency to reduce our time with our Heavenly Father to cold, religious duty. Let's look at natural human relationships as an example. Some couples, though married, make no quality time to spend together – time in which they can talk, share feelings, desires, dreams and disappointments. Rather they get caught up with the demands and pressures of life. Other couples, though they make time to be together, do so more out of duty than love. Hearts never really connect, conversation stays shallow and so the relationship never deepens or strengthens. Then there are couples who, though busy, clear out regular quality time to deepen and grow their relationship. They choose to be "fully present", giving their full attention to the other. Their hearts are laid open before the other and nothing is hidden. This couple spend time both speaking and listening to one another and the result is a deeper, stronger and more intimate relationship.

Our time with God is much the same as this. It is an appointment with the Creator of the universe. He passionately loves you and desires for you to know Him more intimately.

You have a choice to make each day you enter into your meeting with God. Will it be superficial and shallow? Or will you have honest, quality, relational time, a meeting of hearts?

2. Go in open, transparent and vulnerable

"Test me, O Lord, and try me, examine my heart and my mind; for your love is ever before me, and I walk continually in your truth." (Psalm 26:2-3)

"Search me, O God, and know my heart; test me and know my anxious thoughts. See if there is any offensive way in me, and lead me in the way everlasting." (Psalm 139:23-24)

This second ingredient is connected to the first and is also an attitude of the heart – a heart that is open and transparent before the Lord; a heart that says, "I am yours Lord, show me anything that may be offensive to you." It holds nothing back, padlocks no room, but opens wide every door and welcomes the Lord to freely roam through every part of the heart. Like the psalmist who prays the words above, we too must be convinced that our Heavenly Father is all-loving and can be fully trusted with free, unhindered access to our hearts.

Surrender is one of the most beautiful and yet difficult things in any relationship, because risk is involved. The one to whom you open your heart could abuse or hurt it. But without that ongoing trust and openness, the relationship is doomed to stay superficial. You can trust the Lord with your heart and give Him access to every disappointment, every dream and even the sinful things we want no one else to see or find. The Bible says of Jesus, *"A bruised reed he will not break, and a smouldering wick he will not snuff out, till he leads justice to victory"* (Matthew 12:20). He comes in to forgive, heal and restore. I encourage you to pray the two simple prayers above (or something similar in your own words) each time you come to meet with your heavenly Father.

Inevitably, this relational attitude invites the Lord to speak freely, showing us things that need to change, people we may need to forgive or ask forgiveness from, wrongs that may need to be put right. But this is exactly what the Christian life is about – becoming more like Jesus!

3. Keep the Bible as the core of your time

"Jesus answered, It is written: Man does not live on bread alone, but on every word that comes from the mouth of God." (Matthew 4:4)

The Bible is the written Word of God. It is active, alive, powerful, revealing God's will and purpose. It is extremely precious and should be valued highly by all Christians. Over the centuries many people have been killed for translating or transporting the Bible, or simply for possessing one. Today many of us have hard copies, as well as digital ones on phones and computers, written and audio. Yet we may be one of the most undernourished generations.

I have observed an epidemic of sorts. People possess Bibles but don't read them. A new fad seems to have replaced the reading of the Bible: the reading of devotional books! These are normally a short verse followed by a couple paragraphs of explanation by another Christian. This exercise may take all of five minutes and then the believer is satisfied that their religious duty is fulfilled and speed off into their day. This modern and growing trend is one of the causes of weak and powerless believers.

Devotional books can be a useful supplement for those who already have a healthy intake of God's Word – just as vitamins are a useful supplement to a healthy diet. If a person only lived on vitamins, but ate no other food they would eventually die. Not because vitamins are bad, but because a person needs more substantial food. You need more than a couple of verses explained by another person's revelation. You need to read the Word of God for yourself, every day, and in substantial amounts. Your Father not only wants to speak through what others are saying about the Bible, He wants to give you illumination and revelation directly from His Word to your spirit by the power of the Holy Spirit.

"Do not let this Book of the Law depart from your mouth; meditate on it day and night, so that you may be careful to do everything written in it. Then you will be prosperous and

successful." (Joshua 1:8)

It would be helpful for every believer to read the entire Bible through every year. I encourage you to commit to this. There are many Bible reading plans available online or in your Bible itself. Having a plan really helps. I have included one at the back of this book. Here is powerful wisdom in the words of Smith Wigglesworth:

"I understand God by His Word. I cannot understand God by impressions or feelings; I cannot get to know God by sentiments. If I am going to know God, I am going to know Him by His Word. I know I shall be in heaven, but I could not build on my feelings that I am going to heaven. I am going to heaven because God's Word says it, and I believe God's Word. And 'faith cometh by hearing, and hearing by the Word of God' (Romans 10:17). All lack of faith is due to not feeding on God's Word. You need it every day.

How can you enter into a life of faith?

Feed on the living Christ of whom this Word is full. As you get taken up with the glorious fact and the wondrous presence of the living Christ, the faith of God will spring up within you. 'Faith cometh by hearing, and hearing by the Word of God.'"

Remember that the written Word reveals to us the living Word – Jesus. Our reading of the Bible is not what impresses the Lord. God is not impressed by our works, but by the work of Jesus on the cross. Reading the Bible feeds us, changes us and brings knowledge of God's will and purpose for us. It makes a person stronger, wiser and renews our mind to be conformed to God's way of thinking (Romans 12:2)

"Your word is a lamp to my feet and a light for my path." (Psalm 119:105)

I encourage you to read relationally. Smith Wigglesworth said it like this: "Some people read the Bible in Greek and some in Hebrew, but I read it in the Holy Ghost." In other words, you can only read it with the help of the Holy Spirit. He opens up the Scriptures to you. Ask Him to help you understand. Stop as you are reading and pray over those things that are awakened to you or challenge you. This is not a formula, but a living, dynamic relationship. God will meet you in the Holy Scriptures. (I talk in greater detail about how to in-take the Word in my book *Rousing The Warriors*). Let me finish this section with words of wisdom from George Muller:

"The way in which we study this Word is a matter of the deepest moment. The very earliest portion of the day we can command should be devoted to meditation on the Scriptures. Our souls should feed upon the Word. We should read it – not for others, but for ourselves; all the promises, the encouragements, the warnings, the exhortations, the rebukes, should be taken home to our own bosoms. Especially let us remember not to neglect any portion of the Bible: it should be read regularly through. To read favourite portions of the Scriptures, to the exclusion of other parts, is a habit to be avoided. The whole Divine volume is inspired, and by degrees should be read regularly through. But to read the Bible thus is not enough; we must seek to become intimately and (experientially) acquainted with Him whom the Scriptures reveal, with the blessed Jesus who has given Himself to die in our room and stead. Oh, what an abiding, soul-satisfying portion do we possess in Him!"

4. Prayer

Reading the Bible is God speaking to us. But our relationship with Him is two-way and we too must speak with God. This can take many forms. Let me quickly mention five main ones and then focus on how best to use these in your daily time with the Lord.

- Praise – praising or adoring God for who He is
- Worship – a more intimate expression of our loving Him
- Petitions – bringing our needs before Him and asking Him to meet them
- Thanksgiving – the very powerful habit of thanking God
- Repentance – confessing those things we have done wrong and asking for mercy and forgiveness

I don't want to give you a formula, because you need to keep your focus relational. But I would encourage you to think in terms of beginning your encouter time with God by thanking Him, praising and worshipping Him. Then, as you pray and the Lord shows you things that need repentance, be quick to respond and do it with a sincere and earnest heart.

"So I say to you: Ask and it will be given to you; seek and you

will find; knock and the door will be opened to you. For everyone who asks receives; he who seeks finds; and to him who knocks, the door will be opened." (Luke 11:9-10)

Lastly, bring your requests to God. It is not wrong to bring requests to the Lord. He wants and expects us to. But if it is a healthy relationship, then we will focus on Him and what He has already done before we begin to bring new needs to Him. The scripture passage above is taken from the context of Jesus' teaching His disciples to pray. He is telling them to consistently and persistently ask, seek and knock, then it will be done for them. I do believe we need greater faith and boldness in our praying. I encourage you to read the whole passage.

Let me also mention the value and importance of praying in tongues. Jude tells us that we build ourselves up by praying in the Spirit (Jude 20). Paul said that he prayed in tongues more than all the Corinthian church (1 Corinthians 14:18). Every Spirit-filled Christian should use this God-given gift to strengthen and build up their inner man. You should set time aside for this practice and do it with strength, allowing the Spirit of God to pray through you. There are times when we don't know how or what to pray in our natural language and the Holy Spirit will pray through us. This will bring clarity, causing confusion, fear, anxiety and even depression to be dispelled!

There are two more thoughts I want to give you in closing this section. The first is, in all your praying keep listening too. Set aside time to be still and listen to what the Lord is saying to you. He may speak through His Word or impress a thought to you or through a series of circumstances. He speaks through visions, dreams and supernatural experiences too. But develop a listening, inquiring heart. Secondly, don't be formulaic in your praying. Rather than having a set time for prayer, keep it relational. If you are reading the Bible and want to talk to your Father about what you're reading, do it. Keep it fresh and fluid. Allow the Holy Spirit to make these times with Him dynamic.

5. Journal

George Muller said, "Within the last fifty years, I have found it the most profitable plan to meditate with my pen in my hand, writing down the outlines, as the Word is opened to me."

Keeping a journal is a very helpful spiritual discipline in building a relationship with the Lord. It allows us to make a note of the things that the Lord is saying to us in our time with Him. We can record,

- Revelation we receive from His Word
- Promises He is quickening to us for us to believe and hold on to
- A reminder to put something right with a loved one
- Prophetic words
- Written prayers and affections to the Lord
- A record of our prayers and their answers

...and much more. The point really is that we forget quite quickly, but making a note and keeping a record of things is helpful for us. The simple discipline of writing something down helps impress it upon our minds in a deeper way. It also remains there, should we need to look up something later in the day, or a week or even a few months later. This discipline has proven invaluable to me and I encourage everyone to grow in it.

I also use my journal take sermon notes when I am listening to someone. Inevitably something will be said to help me and I know where to look if it is in my journal. It is a good habit to have your journal close at a hand with your Bible, so that even throughout the day you have access to it.

I have used both paper and digital journals. The choice is yours as to what you prefer. You may experiment with both before making up your mind. If done with the right heart and attitude, it becomes something fun that you look forward to. Then, from time to time, you can look back on your journal and remind yourself of your spiritual journey and what the Lord has been saying to you.

Remember not to idolise your daily time with the Lord. It is the act of engaging with Him that is important, not the discipline. One of the enemy's stumbling blocks is to tempt us with pride and it creeps in ever so slyly. We can feel that our continuous effort must be winning "points" with God and perhaps even making us better than other Christians. This subtle entrance of pride is costly and can lead to coldness and confusion, because the Lord resists the proud but gives grace to the humble (James 4:6).

IGNITING THE FLAME

- Our relationship with our Father needs to be nurtured like any other relationship so that it does not grow cold. Determine to do this by have a "daily relational encounter". Use this phrase as a reminder that it should be a) a daily practice, b) relational – we are spending time with someone we love and who loves us and growing to know Him more, and c) an encounter – a living, dynamic, fluid thing, not a dry, religious, repetitive ritual. Use the tools outlined in this chapter to help you make it the former and not the latter.

Come near to the holy men and women of the past and you will soon feel the heat of their desire after God. They mourned for Him, they prayed and wrestled and sought for Him day and night, in season and out, and when they had found Him the finding was all the sweeter for the long seeking.

– AW Tozer

8
Fire Quenchers

I now want to bring a few warnings as I identify the "fire quenchers" – the things that will cause your burning heart to cool rapidly. Much of the book so far has been about things we can do to cultivate our relationship with Jesus and kindle the flame inside. Here we will look briefly at those things we must not do. There are certain attitudes or habits that will quickly extinguish the flames within your heart. They must be avoided at all cost. The Bible commands us to:

"Above all else, guard your heart, for it is the wellspring of life." (Proverbs 4:23)

This is something we need to be very intentional about, because no one else will do it for us. When we read in the Bible, *"Above all else..."* it really means "above all else"! People guard all sorts of precious items they possess using locks, alarms or secret hiding places. But the Lord tells us that the condition of our heart is more precious than anything we may possess – and it must be guarded and protected as our top priority. This is so vital because our heart is the place from which the whole course of our life flows. As we look at the various fire quenchers, think about how you will protect your heart from them, practical ways in which you will build fences to guard yourself.

Avoid pride

The very first fire quencher is the biggest and most dangerous of them all: *pride*. It is also the sin that opens the way for all other sin to enter into our lives and has caused the fall of many mighty people (Proverbs 16:18). Pride kills moves of God. It undermines unity in families and churches. It separates close friends, leading to quarrels and fights. Pride stops honest, open communication and brings distance and coldness. It opens the door to deception and delusion. It must be avoided aggressively at all cost.

I could illustrate each of the examples above with relevant scriptures, but I want to focus our attention on just two major points. The first is: God hates pride and proud people.

"Everyone proud and arrogant in heart is disgusting, hateful, and exceedingly offensive to the Lord; be assured [I pledge it] they will not go unpunished." (Proverbs 16:5 AMP)

This very first truth should be enough for us to deal ruthlessly with pride in our lives. God absolutely and utterly hates pride. Read the verse above again. There are many verses like it in our Bibles. God is not soft or easy on pride because, as the author Charles Bridges put it, "Pride contends for supremacy with God."

Similarly, C.J. Mahaney said, "Pride is when sinful human

beings aspire to the status and position of God and refuse to acknowledge their dependence upon Him."

The second point leads on from the first and that is, God *resists* the proud. Or we could put it this way: God actively opposes the proud. I have heard a preacher say, "I would rather have every demon in hell resist me than God resisting me!" It is a serious thing to have the Lord opposing a person because of their pride. So God both hates and opposes proud people.

"God opposes the proud but gives grace to the humble." (James 4:6)

What are we to do? Pride cannot be cast out of our lives, it must be replaced with humility. Just as much as God hates pride He loves the humble. Just as He actively resists the proud, He is drawn to the humble.

"This is the one I esteem: he who is humble and contrite in spirit, and trembles at my word." (Isaiah 66:2)

The opposite of pride is humility. This is our weapon of choice, a powerful antidote to the venomous poison of pride. Humility attracts the gaze of God towards a person. Grace is freely and richly given to those who choose this difficult but rewarding pathway – a pathway that rewards the humble with riches, honour and life (Proverbs 22:4). Humility stands in stark contradiction to the "spirit of this age" and sadly to many even in the Church who brag on themselves and their achievements. Paul condemns those who "measure themselves by themsevles" and "compare themselves with themselves" as foolish (2

Corinthians 10:12). But it causes demons to tremble and heaven to stand to attention when humans choose the way of humility. It is the nature and attitude that our Saviour was clothed in and that we are commanded to imitate.

"Your attitude should be the same as that of Christ Jesus: Who, being in very nature God, did not consider equality with God something to be grasped, but made himself nothing, taking the very nature of a servant, being made in human likeness." (Philippians 2:5-7)

It also opens the doorway to every other good gift that our Heavenly Father desires to give us. Francis Frangipane puts it beautifully:

"Humility is the door opener to grace: no virtue enters our lives except that humility requests it come."

Humility is a choice not a gift. You must choose this way and culitvate this characteristic in your life. Jesus is our example and the Holy Spirit provides the empowering, but we must still choose to weaken pride and grow in humility. A person cannot become humble once and then have that for the remainder of their lives. The way of humility is a daily walk and a decision. Acknowledge your need of God and His grace daily, give yourself to prayer and the study of his Word. These things express your humility. Look for ways to serve and prefer others. Make yourself accountable to a close friend and ask them to watch out with you for signs of pride. Give them permission to speak into your life and in so doing you are beginning to guard your heart, keeping the flame burning.

Avoid unforgiveness

Harbouring unforgiveness is another big fire quencher. I have met people over the years who have destroyed their own lives and future by holding things against others.

Everyone goes through disappointments in life. Everyone faces rejection at some time or another and inevitably it will come more than once. I am sure that we have all been hurt by others and probably hurt others ourselves. Maybe we have been hurt by the insensitivity of others, broken promises or even outright evil done against us in some way.

I have also observed many people overcome some of the most painful hurts and setbacks. They do this by releasing forgiveness, working through their pain and disappointment and thereby becoming better, bigger people. Sadly, I have also met those who will not forgive. They feel they have a right to hold on to an offence, and because of this a root of bitterness begins to grow like a cancer inside them. They do not realise that it is not only killing them, but effecting everyone close to them. There is no such thing as private sin. The way an individual chooses to live has a direct effect on those around them. I have witnessed whole families infected because of one person's root of bitterness.

"See to it that no one misses the grace of God and that no bitter root grows up to cause trouble and defile many." (Hebrews 12:15)

The Bible has much to say on the subject of forgiveness or the lack of it. Actually, the whole message of Christianity is about forgiveness, beginning with God's forgiveness towards humans who rebelled against Him having turned to selfishness. Let's look at some of Jesus' words on forgiveness.

"For if you forgive men when they sin against you, your heavenly Father will also forgive you. But if you do not forgive men their sins, your Father will not forgive your sins." (Matthew 6:14-15)

Did you realise that according to the words of Jesus Christ that your sins are only forgiven as you forgive those who have sinned against you? This is very important and mostly overlooked by many who have a misguided view of God's grace. As I have travelled and preached around the world, I have met people who believe they are an exception to the words of Jesus, because what they went through was so terrible. But there is no exception. There are not if's or but's in His words. If you do not forgive men their sins, your Father will not forgive your sins. *Selah* (stop and think on that).

The reason our Lord can be so strong about this is because we did not deserve forgiveness and could never earn it. It was offered to us freely. And that which we are given freely must be given freely to others. Jesus really hits this point home by telling the parable of the unforgiving servant in Matthew 18.

What now?

Do you need to forgive anyone? Are you willing to release them?

Forgiveness is a choice, just as unforgiveness is a choice. This may sound too simple, but it is true. You may need to ask the Lord to help you to forgive. I have met people who wanted to forgive, but the pain in their own hearts and memories were too strong. The Lord will help you if this is the case. Sometimes we need to make an initial decision followed by a faith confession, "I forgive them, Father," each time thoughts come to plague you. Depending on the severity of the situation it could take days or weeks for your heart and mind to be healed, but the freedom will come.

True forgiveness releases the other person from the wrong they did and the pain they caused us. True forgiveness chooses not to bring the offence to mind any more.

Paul the Apostle was aware that unforgiveness was a scheme of the devil to trap an individual.

"...I have forgiven in the sight of Christ for your sake, in order that Satan might not outwit us. For we are not unaware of his schemes." (2 Corinthians 2:10-11)

Some need to forgive themselves. Others have harboured things against the Lord and need to let those things go. This is a subject far bigger than space allows me to cover here, but my hope is that you will use these thoughts to avoid unforgiveness and have a constantly forgiving heart.

Avoid isolation

It's interesting to me that Jesus was born into a family and raised with other brothers and sisters. It is also interesting that when He began His ministry, He quickly gathered disciples around Him with whom He lived in true community, doing life together. When Jesus was asked in Matthew 22, what the most important command was, He answered:

"Love the Lord your God with all your heart and with all your soul and with all your mind. This is the first and greatest commandment. And the second is like it: Love your neighbor as yourself. All the Law and the Prophets hang on these two commandments." (Matthew 22:37-40)

This is pretty radical stuff: love God, love people and you fulfil all the Law and the Prophets. Both are relational: a relationship with God and relationships with other people. No man or woman is supposed to be an island. The New Testament Christian message is clearly practiced and lived in the context of community. None of us knows everything and no person has the complete set of gifts. The Lord has set things up in such a way that we need others. We all know in part, see in part (1 Corinthians 13:9) and only as we come together does the bigger picture become clearer. Christians need to live in the context of community with other Christians, sharing and doing life together. It is important to be accountable and hold others to account. For instance, churches in a city or region need the other churches in their area.

Working and living in isolation limits our effectiveness and fruitfulness. The scripture below is well known, but may not be well lived. Read it slowly and prayerfully.

"As it is, there are many parts, but one body. The eye cannot say to the hand, 'I don't need you!' And the head cannot say to the feet, 'I don't need you!' On the contrary, those parts of the body that seem to be weaker are indispensable, and the parts that we think are less honourable we treat with special honour. And the parts that are unpresentable are treated with special modesty, while our presentable parts need no special treatment. But God has combined the members of the body and has given greater honour to the parts that lacked it, so that there should be no division in the body, but that its parts should have equal concern for each other." (1 Corinthians 12:20-25)

We are the Body of Christ and have need of each other. The problem often arises that people find it hard to "do life" with other people. But that is really the point: it is together that we grow and are sanctified. It is together that we best express the Kingdom of God.

"By this will all men know that you are my disciples, that you love one another." (John 13:35)

I am not talking about a soulish, unity movement. I have seen these and they are demonic in nature, because they come from the efforts of man. Anything that originates in our self-life will lead us away from the Kingdom, no matter how good it looks.

The other thing I have observed is that when an individual grows in influence or power, they can be tempted to think they have less need of others. But the opposite is actually true. It is at this very point that an individual needs a community to be a part of, with friends who can speak openly, honestly into their life. Understanding that God has chosen to structure His Kingdom relationally helps us to understand why the enemy seeks to brings division. Rick Joyner says,

"A primary strategy of the enemy is to cause division on every possible level of relationship – churches with churches, congregations and pastors, husbands and wives, parents and children, children with each other."

Be aware of this and order your life in such a way that you live in the context of true community with accountability. I believe every Christian, no matter how gifted or used by the Lord they may be, needs to be part of a church community in which their lives are enriched and roots are entwined with other believers. This will bring health to the individual, but also to the rest of the Body. Consider Paul's advice:

"Instead, we will speak the truth in love, growing in every way more and more like Christ, who is the head of his body, the church. He makes the whole body fit together perfectly. As each part does its own special work, it helps the other parts grow, so that the whole body is healthy and growing and full of love." (Ephesians 4:15-16 NLT)

Avoid the spirit of this age

"Do not be misled: Bad company corrupts good character." (1 Corinthians 15:33)

This last fire quencher may not be as obvious or even spoken of much today, but it is still an area of our lives that we will need to guard against. The term "spirit of this age" refers to the way the world around us thinks and operates; the way it builds friendships, views money handles work etc. When we come to Christ we are called out from those values and ways of thinking. We are told to no longer conform to the pattern of this world but to be transformed. James is really direct when speaking to Christians in his day.

"You adulterous people, don't you know that friendship with the world is hatred toward God? Anyone who chooses to be a friend of the world becomes an enemy of God. Or do you think Scripture says without reason that the spirit he caused to live in us envies intensely?" (James 4:4-5)

This is not speaking to us about segregating our lives from people who are not believers. It is speaking to us to live according to a different set of values – Kingdom values. And wherever the Kingdom and the world clash, we must choose the way of the Kingdom. We could go into many areas and much more detail, but let me focus just on one particular area that has a huge influence upon many lives.

All around us there is a growing trend to be entertained. There are increasingly new and novel ways for that entertainment to be delivered and experienced. It seems to have become an obsession in our culture. Many people work hard, earn good money and then spend much of their time and money on entertainment. It is extremely diverse and seeks the attention and affection of all kinds of people. But some of this depletes our soul and competes with our affection for God. John Piper expresses this truth eloquently:

"The greatest enemy of hunger for God is not poison, but apple pie. It is not the banquet of the wicked that dulls our appetite for heaven, but endless nibbling at the table of the world. It is not the X-rated video, but the prime-time dribble of triviality we drink in every night."

Please don't misunderstand me, hear me out and prayerfully consider if this may apply to your life. I am not against all forms of entertainment, I just believe much of it makes us numb and dulls our spiritual senses. And some of it is an affront to the cross of Christ and the ways of the Kingdom of God. It seems that we have made more and more things "acceptable" in the Church that would not have been acceptable before, on the pretext of them being "culturally relevant".

But as a local Pastor and father I see the problems all around me. Families don't build relationally with each other because hours are spent sitting like zombies in front of a box on a wall. We allow the entertainment industry to parent our children and instil in them values for life and relationships without question or interference. Then some will complain about the behaviour or attitudes of their children!

I believe in recreation over entertainment. A re-creating of energy and replenishing of the soul. This can be done by healthy, wholesome relationship building; doing things together that encourage conversation and intentional dependence. It's uplifting and soul-energising to get out into nature and see it declaring the praises of God. My wife and I have 4 children and we enjoy family life and taking holidays. But we taught ourselves and our children that holidays are "holy days" – a time to be together and enjoy one another, a time to reflect and a time to be with the Lord and enjoy Him.

This is not legalism but a warning to protect your heart and relationship with Jesus. There are no do's or don'ts, but you will need to consider what applies to you, your family, your situation. Then have the courage to change, even though it may be difficult.

Much more could have been said about each of these and perhaps other things that can quench the fire in your heart, but that is for another time. For now, take these short warnings seriously and guard your precious heart against them so that the fire in you can grow and become a raging furnace of God's love to the world around you.

IGNITING THE FLAME

- It is good to focus mostly on the positive aspects of building and nurturing our relationship with God through daily quality time spent with Him, but we must no be ignorant of the devices of the enemy and the ways of the world that would subtley entrap us and extinguish our fire.

- Above all, heed the warning of Scripture to guard your heart and keep your flame burning bright.

He who dwells in the shelter of the Most High
will rest in the shadow of the Almighty.
I will say of the Lord, He is my refuge and my fortress,
my God, in whom I trust.
Surely he will save you from the fowler's snare
and from the deadly pestilence.
He will cover you with his feathers,
and under his wings you will find refuge;
his faithfulness will be your shield and rampart.
You will not fear the terror of night,
nor the arrow that flies by day,
nor the pestilence that stalks in the darkness,
nor the plague that destroys at midday.
A thousand may fall at your side,
ten thousand at your right hand,
but it will not come near you.
You will only observe with your eyes
and see the punishment of the wicked.
If you make the Most High your dwelling
even the Lord, who is my refuge
then no harm will befall you,
no disaster will come near your tent.
For he will command his angels concerning you
to guard you in all your ways;
they will lift you up in their hands,
so that you will not strike your foot against a stone.
You will tread upon the lion and the cobra,
you will trample the great lion and the serpent.
Because he loves me, says the Lord, I will rescue him;
I will protect him, for he acknowledges my name.
He will call upon me, and I will answer him;
I will be with him in trouble,
I will deliver him and honour him.
With long life will I satisfy him and show him my salvation. Psalm 91

9
Abiding In The Secret Place

Even though these are very exciting, hope-filled days for those walking with Jesus, we will also see an increase in darkness and wicked activity. The scripture I quoted earlier in this book from Isaiah 60 speaks both of glorious light and deep darkness. We will see both of these things growing in intensity. There will be great clashes between the two Kingdoms. But those who stay walking close to Jesus will be kept in perfect peace.

"He who dwells in the shelter of the Most High will rest in the shadow of the Almighty. I will say of the Lord, He is my refuge and my fortress, my God, in whom I trust." (Psalm 91:1-2)

The safest place to live or abide is in the secret place of the Most High. It is a place of peace and protection. It is a place where the enemy cannot touch or draw us out. And it is the place the Father has destined for us to live. It is not a geographic place or a house made with hands. It is a spiritual place. But don't be mistaken, it is more real than the book you are holding. Just because you cannot see or explain it physically does not diminish its reality. Throughout history men and women have entered and lived in this place, but it is more imperative now than perhaps at any point in the past.

The thoughts and teaching in this book, if applied, are actually all leading to that place; dying to self, living for Christ, becoming like Christ and creating daily times with Him. These are all helpful pathways to live in the shelter of the Most High. But I felt prompted by the Spirit to make a separate mention of it in concluding this book.

Jesus lived in this rest. He was never rushed, never early and never late. He lived in the perfect peace of the Father. This too is possible for us. It is not easy, but it really is available. I believe that there is much grace available for those who will pursue this pathway. Though it sounds like a contradiction, it takes effort to enter this rest. Look with me at Hebrews 4. The whole chapter is worth reading, but let me just quote a few verses.

"There remains, then, a Sabbath-rest for the people of God; for anyone who enters God's rest also rests from his own work, just as God did from his. Let us, therefore, make every effort to enter that rest, so that no one will fall by following their example of disobedience." (Hebrews 4:9-11)

The reason you will need to make every effort is because the world around you is wired in such a way as to entice or draw you out of that place of rest with the Father. Over the last few years

I have entered into this place for short periods, but am believing for those periods to grow and extend until it becomes an abiding place. The abiding place is the Lord's desire for all His children.

"You will keep him in perfect peace,

Whose mind is stayed on You,

Because he trusts in You." (Isaiah 26:2 NKJV)

There are two simple, practical steps you can take to enter this rest. Firstly, trust the Lord at all times and in all situations. Sometimes this is easier said than done, but it is not impossible for the diligent seeker and follower.

Secondly, learn to keep your mind stayed on Him. The message of this book is actually leading you to do both of these things. You can cultivate this by developing a habit of committing some key scriptures to memory and using them to bring your trust back upon the Lord (such as Psalm 27 below).

"The Lord is my light and my salvation –

whom shall I fear?

The Lord is the stronghold of my life –

of whom shall I be afraid?

When evil men advance against me

to devour my flesh,

When my enemies and my foes attack me,

they will stumble and fall.

Though an army besiege me,

my heart will not fear;

Though war break out against me,

even then will I be confident.
One thing I ask of the Lord,
this is what I seek:
That I may dwell in the house of the Lord
all the days of my life,
to gaze upon the beauty of the Lord
and to seek him in his temple.
For in the day of trouble
he will keep me safe in his dwelling;
he will hide me in the shelter of his tabernacle
and set me high upon a rock." (Psalm 27:1-5)

My prayers are with you. Perhaps our paths will cross, but if not on earth, then we will rejoice together in heaven one day. Join the growing Company of Burning Hearts on the earth today!

Appendix: The Emperor's New Clothes

Once upon a time there lived a vain Emperor whose only worry in life was to dress in elegant clothes. He changed clothes almost every hour and loved to show them off to his people.

Word of the Emperor's refined habits spread over his kingdom and beyond. Two scoundrels who had heard of the Emperor's vanity decided to take advantage of it. They introduced themselves at the gates of the palace with a scheme in mind.

"We are two very good tailors and after many years of research we have invented an extraordinary method to weave a cloth so light and fine that it looks invisible. As a matter of fact it is invisible to anyone who is too stupid and incompetent to appreciate its quality."

The chief of the guards heard the scoundrel's strange story and sent for the court chamberlain. The chamberlain notified the prime minister, who ran to the Emperor and disclosed the incredible news. The Emperor's curiosity got the better of him and he decided to see the two scoundrels.

"Besides being invisible, your Highness, this cloth will be woven in colours and patterns created especially for you." The emperor gave the two men a bag of gold coins in exchange for their promise to begin working on the fabric immediately.

"Just tell us what you need to get started and we'll give it to you." The two scoundrels asked for a loom, silk, gold thread and then pretended to begin working. The Emperor thought he had spent his money quite well: in addition to getting a new extraordinary suit, he would discover which of his subjects were ignorant and incompetent. A few days later, he called the old and wise prime minister, who was considered by everyone as a man with common sense.

"Go and see how the work is proceeding," the Emperor told him, "and come back to let me know."

The prime minister was welcomed by the two scoundrels.

"We're almost finished, but we need a lot more gold thread. Here, Excellency! Admire the colors, feel the softness!" The old man bent over the loom and tried to see the fabric that was not there. He felt cold sweat on his forehead.

"I can't see anything," he thought. "If I see nothing, that means I'm stupid! Or, worse, incompetent!" If the prime minister admitted that he didn't see anything, he would be discharged from his office. "What a marvellous fabric," he said then. "I'll certainly tell the Emperor." The two scoundrels rubbed their hands gleefully. They had almost made it. More thread was requested to finish the work.

Finally, the Emperor received the announcement that the two tailors had come to take all the measurements needed to sew his new suit.

"Come in," the Emperor ordered. Even as they bowed, the two scoundrels pretended to be holding large roll of fabric.

"Here it is your Highness, the result of our labour," the scoundrels said. "We have worked night and day but, at last, the most beautiful fabric in the world is ready for you. Look at the colours and feel how fine it is." Of course the Emperor did not see any colours and could not feel any cloth between his fingers. He panicked and felt like fainting. But luckily the throne was right behind him and he sat down. But when he realized that no one could know that he did not see the fabric, he felt better. Nobody could find out he was stupid and incompetent. And the Emperor didn't know that everybody else around him thought and did the very same thing.

The farce continued as the two scoundrels had foreseen it. Once they had taken the measurements, the two began cutting the air with scissors while sewing with their needles an invisible cloth.

"Your Highness, you'll have to take off your clothes to try on your new ones." The two scoundrels draped the new clothes on him and then held up a mirror. The Emperor was embarrassed but since none of his bystanders were, he felt relieved.

"Yes, this is a beautiful suit and it looks very good on me," the Emperor said trying to look comfortable. "You've done a fine job."

"Your Majesty," the prime minister said, "we have a request for you. The people have found out about this extraordinary fabric and they are anxious to see you in your new suit." The Emperor was doubtful showing himself naked to the people, but then he abandoned his fears. After all, no one would know about it except the ignorant and the incompetent.

"All right," he said. "I will grant the people this privilege." He summoned his carriage and the ceremonial parade was formed. A group of dignitaries walked at the very front of the procession and anxiously scrutinized the faces of the people in the street. All the people had gathered in the main square, pushing and shoving to get a better look. An applause welcomed the regal procession. Everyone wanted to know how stupid or incompetent his or her neighbour was but, as the Emperor passed, a strange murmur rose from the crowd.

Everyone said, loud enough for the others to hear: "Look at the Emperor's new clothes. They're beautiful!"

"What a marvellous train!"

"And the colours! The colours of that beautiful fabric! I have never seen anything like it in my life!" They all tried to conceal their disappointment at not being able to see the clothes, and since nobody was willing to admit his own stupidity and incompetence, they all behaved as the two scoundrels had predicted.

142

A child, however, who had no important job and could only see things as his eyes showed them to him, went up to the carriage.

"The Emperor is naked," he said.

"Fool!" his father reprimanded, running after him. "Don't talk nonsense!" He grabbed his child and took him away. But the boy's remark, which had been heard by the bystanders, was repeated over and over again until everyone cried:

"The boy is right! The Emperor is naked! It's true!"

The Emperor realised that the people were right but could not admit to that. He though it better to continue the procession under the illusion that anyone who couldn't see his clothes was either stupid or incompetent. And he stood stiffly on his carriage, while behind him a page held his imaginary mantle.

Company Of Burning Hearts
– the vision

Company of Burning Hearts (COBH) was birthed out of a direct word from the Lord to prepare for the coming move of God. I had just finished praying for some people who had been dry, but hungry and they experienced a saturating in the mighty presence of God. As I walked away the Lord spoke clearly to my heart, "I am raising a company of burning hearts." Though I did not hear an audible voice, I felt the significance of the phrase the Holy Spirit had just quickened to me. *Company of Burning Hearts.* It reverberated through me and I felt the Lord saying He has many whose hearts are being set aflame for Jesus. There are also those who have a deep yearning within them, knowing that there must be more than they currently live in, but they have not experienced it yet. They feel like ground that is dry, cracked and longing for the rains of His presence to fall upon them and saturate them. This is why this ministry exists, to answer that cry.

Men, women and children have been responding to the drawing of the Holy Spirit. It may still be small and just beginning, but this company will become a mighty force. These Holy Ones will manifest the power and nature of Jesus. They will be from all walks of life, young and old, men and women, boys and girls. Their lives, their words, will all manifest the Kingdom of God, bringing hope and love to many.

Walking with Jesus

"Did not our hearts burn within us when he talked to us." (Luke 24:32)

The phrase is taken from Luke's gospel when the two disciples walked with Jesus. Every heart was created to burn, to be aflame, to be alive, overflowing with the radiating glory of His divine presence. Adam and Eve lived in the atmosphere of that glory. Enoch walked so closely with God that he never experienced death, but was translated from this earthly realm to heaven. Humans were created to house the Divine. To live in communion with our Maker is not a pipe-dream. Because of the work of Jesus on the cross it can be a reality now. Too many have settled way below God's best, allowing their lives to be lived in mediocrity, often captivated by temporal things. COBH seeks to unite like-spirited people, fuelling their fire to make it even stronger for Jesus.

COBH has three aims:

Ignite – Set on Fire by Jesus' Love

"In reply Jesus declared, I tell you the truth, no one can see the kingdom of God unless he is born again." (John 3:3)

This is were it all begins, when a person comes to Christ and acknowledges Him as their Lord and Saviour. The Bible says that they become a brand new creation and all the old is removed. We want to see thousands of people have the fire of salvation ignited in them.

Awake – Empowered by the Holy Spirit

"But after me will come one who is more powerful than I ... He will baptise you with the Holy Spirit and with fire." (Matthew 3:11)

Holy Spirit baptism is not only available for every one who believes upon Jesus, but is needed to be able to live the Life God has called us to. We are committed to seeing people walk in the full power of the Holy Spirit.

Fuel – Sustaining the Fire

"His word is in my heart like a fire, a fire shut up in my bones." (Jeremiah 20:9). Every fire needs fuel to keep burning and also needs to be protected against the elements. We are committed to providing tools to help fuel a person's fire for the Lord. This will be through online teaching, gathered events, books and resources. See **www.companyofburninghearts.net**

COMPANY OF **BURNING HEARTS**

IGNITE ○ AWAKE ○ FUEL

Bible Reading Plan

January

	New Testament		Old Testament	
	▸ MATTHEW	**▸ ACTS**	**▸ PSALMS**	**▸ GENESIS**
1.	☐ 1:1-17	☐ 1:1-11	☐ 1	☐ 1-2
2.	☐ 1:18-25	☐ 1:12-26	☐ 2	☐ 3-4
3.	☐ 2:1-12	☐ 2:1-21	☐ 3	☐ 5-8
4.	☐ 2:13-23	☐ 2:22-47	☐ 4	☐ 9-11
5.	☐ 3:1-12	☐ 3	☐ 5	☐ 12-14
6.	☐ 3:13-17	☐ 4:1-22	☐ 6	☐ 15-17
7.	☐ 4:1-11	☐ 4:23-37	☐ 7	☐ 18-20
8.	☐ 4:12-17	☐ 5:1-16	☐ 8	☐ 21-23
9.	☐ 4:18-25	☐ 5:17-42	☐ 9	☐ 24
10.	☐ 5:1-12	☐ 6	☐ 10	☐ 25-26
11.	☐ 5:13-20	☐ 7:1-38	☐ 11	☐ 27-28
12.	☐ 5:21-32	☐ 7:39-60	☐ 12	☐ 29-30
13.	☐ 5:33-48	☐ 8:1-25	☐ 13	☐ 31
14.	☐ 6:1-15	☐ 8:26-40	☐ 14	☐ 32-33
15.	☐ 6:16-24	☐ 9:1-19	☐ 15	☐ 34-35
16.	☐ 6:25-34	☐ 9:20-43	☐ 16	☐ 36
17.	☐ 7:1-14	☐ 10:1-23	☐ 17	☐ 37-38
18.	☐ 7:15-29	☐ 10:24-48	☐ 18:1-24	☐ 39-40
19.	☐ 8:1-13	☐ 11:1-18	☐ 18:25-50	☐ 41
20.	☐ 8:14-22	☐ 11:19-30	☐ 19	☐ 42-43
21.	☐ 8:23-34	☐ 12	☐ 20	☐ 44-45
22.	☐ 9:1-13	☐ 13:1-25	☐ 21	☐ 46-47
23.	☐ 9:14-26	☐ 13:26-52	☐ 22:1-11	☐ 48
24.	☐ 9:27-38	☐ 14	☐ 22:12-31	☐ 49
25.	☐ 10:1-20	☐ 15:1-21	☐ 23	☐ 50

February

	New Testament		**Old Testament**	
	▸ **MATTHEW**	▸ **ACTS**	▸ **PSALMS**	▸ **EXODUS**
1.	☐ 10:21-42	☐ 15:22-41	☐ 24	☐ 1-3
2.	☐ 11:1-19	☐ 16:1-15	☐ 25	☐ 4-6
3.	☐ 11:20-30	☐ 16:16-40	☐ 26	☐ 7-9
4.	☐ 12:1-21	☐ 17:1-15	☐ 27	☐ 10-12
5.	☐ 12:22-37	☐ 17:16-34	☐ 28	☐ 13-15
6.	☐ 12:38-50	☐ 18:1-17	☐ 29	☐ 16-18
7.	☐ 13:1-23	☐ 18:18-28	☐ 30	☐ 19-20
8.	☐ 13:24-43	☐ 19:1-22	☐ 31	☐ 21-23
9.	☐ 13:44-58	☐ 19:23-41	☐ 32	☐ 24-26
10.	☐ 14:1-21	☐ 20:1-12	☐ 33	☐ 27-29
11.	☐ 14:22-36	☐ 20:13-38	☐ 34	☐ 30-31
12.	☐ 15:1-20	☐ 21:1-26	☐ 35	☐ 32-33
13.	☐ 15:21-39	☐ 21:27-40	☐ 36	☐ 34
14.	☐ 16:1-12	☐ 22	☐ 37:1-22	☐ 35-37
15.	☐ 16:13-28	☐ 23:1-11	☐ 37:23-40	☐ 38-40
				▸ **LEVITICUS**
16.	☐ 17:1-13	☐ 23:12-35	☐ 38	☐ 1-4
17.	☐ 17:14-27	☐ 24	☐ 39	☐ 5-7
18.	☐ 18:1-14	☐ 25:1-12	☐ 40	☐ 8-10
19.	☐ 18:15-35	☐ 25:13-27	☐ 41	☐ 11-13
20.	☐ 19:1-15	☐ 26:1-18	☐ 42	☐ 14-15
21.	☐ 19:16-30	☐ 26:19-32	☐ 43	☐ 16-17
22.	☐ 20:1-16	☐ 27:1-26	☐ 44	☐ 18-20
23.	☐ 20:17-34	☐ 27:27-44	☐ 45	☐ 21-23
24.	☐ 21:1-11	☐ 28:1-16	☐ 46	☐ 24-25
25.	☐ 21:12-22	☐ 28:17-31	☐ 47	☐ 26-27

March

	New Testament		Old Testament	
	▸ MATTHEW	**▸ ROMANS**	**▸ PSALMS**	**▸ NUMBERS**
1.	☐ 21:23-32	☐ 1:1-17	☐ 48	☐ 1-2
2.	☐ 21:33-46	☐ 1:18-32	☐ 49	☐ 3-4
3.	☐ 22:1-14	☐ 2	☐ 50	☐ 5-6
4.	☐ 22:15-33	☐ 3	☐ 51	☐ 7-8
5.	☐ 22:34-46	☐ 4	☐ 52	☐ 9-11
6.	☐ 23:1-12	☐ 5:1-11	☐ 53	☐ 12-14
7.	☐ 23:13-24	☐ 5:12-21	☐ 54	☐ 15-17
8.	☐ 23:25-39	☐ 6:1-14	☐ 55	☐ 18-20
9.	☐ 24:1-14	☐ 6:15-23	☐ 56	☐ 21-22
10.	☐ 24:15-35	☐ 7:1-12	☐ 57	☐ 23-25
11.	☐ 24:36-51	☐ 7:13-25	☐ 58	☐ 26-27
12.	☐ 25:1-13	☐ 8:1-17	☐ 59	☐ 28-30
13.	☐ 25:14-30	☐ 8:18-39	☐ 60	☐ 31-32
14.	☐ 25:31-46	☐ 9:1-18	☐ 61	☐ 33-36
				▸ DEUT.
15.	☐ 26:1-16	☐ 9:19-33	☐ 62	☐ 1-3
16.	☐ 26:17-35	☐ 10	☐ 63	☐ 4-5
17.	☐ 26:36-56	☐ 11:1-24	☐ 64	☐ 6-8
18.	☐ 26:57-75	☐ 11:25-36	☐ 65	☐ 9-12
19.	☐ 27:1-10	☐ 12:1-8	☐ 66	☐ 13-17
20.	☐ 27:11-26	☐ 12:9-21	☐ 67	☐ 18-21
21.	☐ 27:27-44	☐ 13	☐ 68	☐ 22-26
22.	☐ 27:45-56	☐ 14	☐ 69:1-18	☐ 27-28
23.	☐ 27:57-66	☐ 15:1-13	☐ 69:19-36	☐ 29-31
24.	☐ 28:1-10	☐ 15:14-33	☐ 70	☐ 32
25.	☐ 28:11-20	☐ 16	☐ 71	☐ 33-34

April

	New Testament		Old Testament	
	▸ MARK	**▸ 1 COR.**	**▸ PSALMS**	**▸ JOSHUA**
1.	☐ 1:1-8	☐ 1:1-17	☐ 72	☐ 1-2
2.	☐ 1:9-20	☐ 1:18-31	☐ 73	☐ 3-5
3.	☐ 1:21-34	☐ 2	☐ 74	☐ 6-7
4.	☐ 1:35-45	☐ 3	☐ 75	☐ 8-9
5.	☐ 2:1-12	☐ 4	☐ 76	☐ 10-12
6.	☐ 2:13-17	☐ 5	☐ 77	☐ 13-14
7.	☐ 2:18-28	☐ 6:1-11	☐ 78:1-39	☐ 15-17
8.	☐ 3:1-19	☐ 6:12-20	☐ 78:40-72	☐ 18-19
9.	☐ 3:20-35	☐ 7:1-16	☐ 79	☐ 20-21
10.	☐ 4:1-20	☐ 7:17-40	☐ 80	☐ 22-23
11.	☐ 4:21-41	☐ 8	☐ 81	☐ 24
				▸ JUDGES
12.	☐ 5:1-20	☐ 9:1-12	☐ 82	☐ 1-3
13.	☐ 5:21-43	☐ 9:13-27	☐ 83	☐ 4-5
14.	☐ 6:1-13	☐ 10:1-13	☐ 84	☐ 6-7
15.	☐ 6:14-29	☐ 10:14-33	☐ 85	☐ 8
16.	☐ 6:30-44	☐ 11:1-16	☐ 86	☐ 9
17.	☐ 6:45-56	☐ 11:17-34	☐ 87	☐ 10-12
18.	☐ 7:1-23	☐ 12:1-13	☐ 88	☐ 13-15
19.	☐ 7:24-37	☐ 12:14-31	☐ 89:1-18	☐ 16
20.	☐ 8:1-13	☐ 13	☐ 89:19-52	☐ 17-18
21.	☐ 8:14-21	☐ 14:1-25	☐ 90	☐ 19
22.	☐ 8:22-30	☐ 14:26-40	☐ 91	☐ 20-21
				▸ RUTH
23.	☐ 8:31-38	☐ 15:1-28	☐ 92	☐ 1
24.	☐ 9:1-13	☐ 15:29-58	☐ 93	☐ 2-3
25.	☐ 9:14-32	☐ 16	☐ 94	☐ 4

May

	New Testament		**Old Testament**	
	▶ **MARK**	▶ **2 COR.**	▶ **PSALMS**	▶ **1 SAMUEL**
1.	☐ 9:33-50	☐ 1:1-11	☐ 95	☐ 1-2
2.	☐ 10:1-16	☐ 1:12-24	☐ 96	☐ 3-5
3.	☐ 10:17-34	☐ 2	☐ 97	☐ 6-8
4.	☐ 10:35-52	☐ 3	☐ 98	☐ 9-10
5.	☐ 11:1-11	☐ 4	☐ 99	☐ 11-13
6.	☐ 11:12-26	☐ 5	☐ 100	☐ 14
7.	☐ 11:27-33	☐ 6	☐ 101	☐ 15-16
8.	☐ 12:1-12	☐ 7	☐ 102	☐ 17-18
9.	☐ 12:13-27	☐ 8	☐ 103	☐ 19-20
10.	☐ 12:28-34	☐ 9	☐ 104	☐ 21-23
11.	☐ 12:35-44	☐ 10	☐ 105	☐ 24-25
12.	☐ 13:1-13	☐ 11:1-15	☐ 106:1-23	☐ 26-28
13.	☐ 13:14-31	☐ 11:16-33	☐ 106:24-48	☐ 29-31
				▶ **2 SAMUEL**
14.	☐ 13:32-37	☐ 12:1-10	☐ 107	☐ 1-2
15.	☐ 14:1-11	☐ 12:11-21	☐ 108	☐ 3-4
16.	☐ 14:12-31	☐ 13	☐ 109	☐ 5-7
		▶ **GALATIANS**		
17.	☐ 14:32-42	☐ 1	☐ 110	☐ 8-10
18.	☐ 14:43-52	☐ 2	☐ 111	☐ 11-12
19.	☐ 14:53-65	☐ 3:1-14	☐ 112	☐ 13
20.	☐ 14:66-72	☐ 3:15-29	☐ 113	☐ 14-15
21.	☐ 15:1-15	☐ 4:1-20	☐ 114	☐ 16-17
22.	☐ 15:16-32	☐ 4:21-31	☐ 115	☐ 18-19
23.	☐ 15:33-41	☐ 5:1-12	☐ 116	☐ 20-21
24.	☐ 15:42-47	☐ 5:13-26	☐ 117	☐ 22
25.	☐ 16	☐ 6	☐ 118	☐ 23-24

June

	New Testament		Old Testament	
	▶ **LUKE**	▶ **EPHESIANS**	▶ **PSALMS**	▶ **1 KINGS**
1.	☐ 1:1-25	☐ 1:1-14	☐ 119:1-8	☐ 1
2.	☐ 1:26-38	☐ 1:15-23	☐ 119:9-16	☐ 2-3
3.	☐ 1:39-56	☐ 2:1-10	☐ 119:17-24	☐ 4-5
4.	☐ 1:57-66	☐ 2:11-22	☐ 119:25-32	☐ 6-7
5.	☐ 1:67-80	☐ 3:1-13	☐ 119:33-40	☐ 8
6.	☐ 2:1-20	☐ 3:14-21	☐ 119:41-48	☐ 9-10
7.	☐ 2:21-40	☐ 4:1-16	☐ 119:49-56	☐ 11
8.	☐ 2:41-52	☐ 4:17-24	☐ 119:57-64	☐ 12
9.	☐ 3:1-20	☐ 4:25-32	☐ 119:65-72	☐ 13-14
10.	☐ 3:21-38	☐ 5:1-21	☐ 119:73-80	☐ 15-16
11.	☐ 4:1-12	☐ 5:22-33	☐ 119:81-88	☐ 17-18
12.	☐ 4:13-30	☐ 6:1-9	☐ 119:89-96	☐ 19-20
13.	☐ 4:31-37	☐ 6:10-24	☐ 119:97-104	☐ 21-22
		▶ **PHILIPPIANS**		▶ **2 KINGS**
14.	☐ 4:38-44	☐ 1:1-11	☐ 119:105-112	☐ 1-3
15.	☐ 5:1-11	☐ 1:12-20	☐ 119:113-120	☐ 4-5
16.	☐ 5:12-16	☐ 1:21-30	☐ 119:121-128	☐ 6-7
17.	☐ 5:17-26	☐ 2:1-11	☐ 119:129-136	☐ 8-9
18.	☐ 5:27-32	☐ 2:12-18	☐ 119:137-144	☐ 10-11
19.	☐ 5:33-39	☐ 2:19-30	☐ 119:145-152	☐ 12-13
20.	☐ 6:1-16	☐ 3:1-9	☐ 119:153-160	☐ 14-15
21.	☐ 6:17-26	☐ 3:10-14	☐ 119:161-168	☐ 16-17
22.	☐ 6:27-36	☐ 3:15-21	☐ 119:169-176	☐ 18-19
23.	☐ 6:37-42	☐ 4:1-7	☐ 120	☐ 20-21
24.	☐ 6:43-49	☐ 4:8-13	☐ 121	☐ 22-23
25.	☐ 7:1-10	☐ 4:14-23	☐ 122	☐ 24-25

July

	New Testament		**Old Testament**	
	▸LUKE	**▸COLOSSIANS**	**▸PSALMS**	**▸1 CHRON.**
1.	☐ 7:11-17	☐ 1:1-14	☐ 123-124	☐ 1-2
2.	☐ 7:18-35	☐ 1:15-29	☐ 125	☐ 3-4
3.	☐ 7:36-50	☐ 2:1-7	☐ 126	☐ 5-6
4.	☐ 8:1-15	☐ 2:8-15	☐ 127	☐ 7-9
5.	☐ 8:16-25	☐ 2:16-23	☐ 128	☐ 10-11
6.	☐ 8:26-39	☐ 3:1-14	☐ 129	☐ 12-14
7.	☐ 8:40-56	☐ 3:15-25	☐ 130-131	☐ 15-16
8.	☐ 9:1-17	☐ 4:1-9	☐ 132	☐ 17-19
9.	☐ 9:18-27	☐ 4:10-18	☐ 133-134	☐ 20-22
		▸1 THESSALONIANS		
10.	☐ 9:28-36	☐ 1	☐ 135	☐ 23-25
11.	☐ 9:37-50	☐ 2:1-9	☐ 136	☐ 26-28
12.	☐ 9:51-62	☐ 2:10-20	☐ 137	☐ 29
				▸2 CHRON.
13.	☐ 10:1-16	☐ 3:1-6	☐ 138	☐ 1-2
14.	☐ 10:17-24	☐ 3:7-13	☐ 139	☐ 3-5
15.	☐ 10:25-37	☐ 4:1-10	☐ 140	☐ 6-7
16.	☐ 10:38-42	☐ 4:11-18	☐ 141	☐ 8-9
17.	☐ 11:1-13	☐ 5:1-11	☐ 142	☐ 10-12
18.	☐ 11:14-28	☐ 5:12-28	☐ 143	☐ 13-16
		▸2 THESSALONIANS		
19.	☐ 11:29-36	☐ 1:1-7	☐ 144	☐ 17-19
20.	☐ 11:37-54	☐ 1:8-12	☐ 145	☐ 20-21
21.	☐ 12:1-12	☐ 2:1-12	☐ 146	☐ 22-24
22.	☐ 12:13-21	☐ 2:13-17	☐ 147	☐ 25-27
23.	☐ 12:22-34	☐ 3:1-5	☐ 148	☐ 28-29
24.	☐ 12:35-48	☐ 3:6-13	☐ 149	☐ 30-33
25.	☐ 12:49-59	☐ 3:14-18	☐ 150	☐ 34-36

August

	New Testament		**Old Testament**	
	▸ **LUKE**	▸ **1 TIMOTHY**	▸ **PROVERBS**	▸ **EZRA**
1.	☐ 13:1-9	☐ 1:1-11	☐ 1	☐ 1-2
2.	☐ 13:10-21	☐ 1:12-20	☐ 2	☐ 3
3.	☐ 13:22-35	☐ 2	☐ 3	☐ 4-5
4.	☐ 14:1-14	☐ 3:1-10	☐ 4	☐ 6
5.	☐ 14:15-24	☐ 3:11-16	☐ 5	☐ 7
6.	☐ 14:25-35	☐ 4	☐ 6	☐ 8
7.	☐ 15:1-10	☐ 5:1-15	☐ 7	☐ 9
8.	☐ 15:11-32	☐ 5:16-25	☐ 8	☐ 10
				▸ **NEH.**
9.	☐ 16:1-9	☐ 6:1-10	☐ 9	☐ 1-2
10.	☐ 16:10-18	☐ 6:11-21	☐ 10:1-16	☐ 3
		▸ **2 TIMOTHY**		
11.	☐ 16:19-31	☐ 1:1-7	☐ 10:17-32	☐ 4-5
12.	☐ 17:1-10	☐ 1:8-18	☐ 11:1-15	☐ 6
13.	☐ 17:11-19	☐ 2:1-13	☐ 11:16-31	☐ 7
14.	☐ 17:20-37	☐ 2:14-26	☐ 12:1-14	☐ 8
15.	☐ 18:1-8	☐ 3:1-9	☐ 12:15-28	☐ 9
16.	☐ 18:9-17	☐ 3:10-17	☐ 13:1-12	☐ 10
17.	☐ 18:18-30	☐ 4	☐ 13:13-25	☐ 11
		▸ **TITUS**		
18.	☐ 18:31-43	☐ 1:1-9	☐ 14:1-18	☐ 12
19.	☐ 19:1-10	☐ 1:10-16	☐ 14:19-35	☐ 13
				▸ **ESTHER**
20.	☐ 19:11-27	☐ 2:1-10	☐ 15:1-17	☐ 1
21.	☐ 19:28-38	☐ 2:11-15	☐ 15:18-33	☐ 2
22.	☐ 19:39-48	☐ 3:1-8	☐ 16:1-16	☐ 3-4
23.	☐ 20:1-8	☐ 3:9-15	☐ 16:17-33	☐ 5-6
		▸ **PHILEMON**		
24.	☐ 20:9-19	☐ 1-11	☐ 17:1-14	☐ 7-8
25.	☐ 20:20-26	☐ 12-25	☐ 17:15-28	☐ 9-10

September

	New Testament		**Old Testament**	
	▸ LUKE	**▸ HEBREWS**	**▸ PROVERBS**	**▸ ISAIAH**
1.	☐ 20:27-40	☐ 1:1-9	☐ 18	☐ 1-2
2.	☐ 20:41-47	☐ 1:10-14	☐ 19:1-14	☐ 3-5
3.	☐ 21:1-19	☐ 2:1-9	☐ 19:15-29	☐ 6-8
4.	☐ 21:20-28	☐ 2:10-18	☐ 20:1-15	☐ 9-10
5.	☐ 21:29-38	☐ 3	☐ 20:16-30	☐ 11-13
6.	☐ 22:1-13	☐ 4:1-11	☐ 21:1-16	☐ 14-16
7.	☐ 22:14-23	☐ 4:12-16	☐ 21:17-31	☐ 17-20
8.	☐ 22:24-30	☐ 5	☐ 22:1-16	☐ 21-23
9.	☐ 22:31-38	☐ 6:1-12	☐ 22:17-29	☐ 24-26
10.	☐ 22:39:46	☐ 6:13-20	☐ 23:1-18	☐ 27-28
11.	☐ 22:47-53	☐ 7:1-10	☐ 23:19-35	☐ 29-30
12.	☐ 22:54-62	☐ 7:11-28	☐ 24:1-22	☐ 31-33
13.	☐ 22:63-71	☐ 8:1-6	☐ 24:23-34	☐ 34-36
14.	☐ 23:1-12	☐ 8:7-13	☐ 25:1-14	☐ 37-39
15.	☐ 23:13-25	☐ 9:1-10	☐ 25:15-28	☐ 40-41
16.	☐ 23:26-31	☐ 9:11-28	☐ 26:1-16	☐ 42-43
17.	☐ 23:32-37	☐ 10:1-18	☐ 26:17-28	☐ 44-45
18.	☐ 23:38-43	☐ 10:19-39	☐ 27:1-14	☐ 46-48
19.	☐ 23:44-49	☐ 11:1-16	☐ 27:15-27	☐ 49-50
20.	☐ 23:50-56	☐ 11:17-31	☐ 28:1-14	☐ 51-53
21.	☐ 24:1-12	☐ 11:32-40	☐ 28:15-28	☐ 54-55
22.	☐ 24:13-27	☐ 12:1-13	☐ 29:1-14	☐ 56-58
23.	☐ 24:28-35	☐ 12:14-29	☐ 29:15-27	☐ 59-61
24.	☐ 24:36-44	☐ 13:1-8	☐ 30	☐ 62-64
25.	☐ 24:45-53	☐ 13:9-25	☐ 31	☐ 65-66

October

	New Testament		*Old Testament*	
	▸ JOHN	**▸ JAMES**	**▸ ECCLES.**	**▸ JEREMIAH**
1.	☐ 1:1-18	☐ 1:1-11	☐ 1	☐ 1-2
2.	☐ 1:19-28	☐ 1:12-18	☐ 2:1-16	☐ 3-4
3.	☐ 1:29-34	☐ 1:19-27	☐ 2:17-26	☐ 5-6
4.	☐ 1:35-42	☐ 2:1-13	☐ 3:1-15	☐ 7-9
5.	☐ 1:43-51	☐ 2:14-26	☐ 3:16-22	☐ 10-11
6.	☐ 2:1-11	☐ 3:1-12	☐ 4	☐ 12-13
7.	☐ 2:12-25	☐ 3:13-18	☐ 5	☐ 14-15
8.	☐ 3:1-15	☐ 4:1-10	☐ 6	☐ 16-18
9.	☐ 3:16-21	☐ 4:11-17	☐ 7:1-14	☐ 19-22
10.	☐ 3:22-36	☐ 5:1-6	☐ 7:15-29	☐ 23-25
11.	☐ 4:1-14	☐ 5:7-12	☐ 8	☐ 26-29
12.	☐ 4:15-26	☐ 5:13-20	☐ 9	☐ 30-31
		▸ 1 PETER		
13.	☐ 4:27-42	☐ 1:1-9	☐ 10	☐ 32-34
14.	☐ 4:43-54	☐ 1:10-16	☐ 11	☐ 35-38
15.	☐ 5:1-15	☐ 1:17-25	☐ 12	☐ 39-43
			▸ SONG OF SONGS	
16.	☐ 5:16-30	☐ 2:1-8	☐ 1	☐ 44-46
17.	☐ 5:31-47	☐ 2:9-17	☐ 2	☐ 47-48
18.	☐ 6:1-15	☐ 2:18-25	☐ 3	☐ 49
19.	☐ 6:16-24	☐ 3:1-7	☐ 4:1-7	☐ 50
20.	☐ 6:25-40	☐ 3:8-12	☐ 4:8-16	☐ 51
21.	☐ 6:41-59	☐ 3:13-22	☐ 5	☐ 52
				▸ LAM.
22.	☐ 6:60-71	☐ 4:1-11	☐ 6	☐ 1
23.	☐ 7:1-13	☐ 4:12-19	☐ 7	☐ 2
24.	☐ 7:14-24	☐ 5:1-7	☐ 8:1-7	☐ 3
25.	☐ 7:25-36	☐ 5:8-14	☐ 8:8-14	☐ 4-5

November

	New Testament		**Old Testament**	
	▸ **JOHN**	▸ **2 PETER**	▸ **JOB**	▸ **EZEKIEL**
1.	☐ 7:37-44	☐ 1:1-11	☐ 1	☐ 1-3
2.	☐ 7:45-53	☐ 1:12-21	☐ 2	☐ 4-8
3.	☐ 8:1-11	☐ 2:1-9	☐ 3	☐ 9-12
4.	☐ 8:12-20	☐ 2:10-16	☐ 4	☐ 13-15
5.	☐ 8:21-30	☐ 2:17-22	☐ 5	☐ 16
6.	☐ 8:31-47	☐ 3:1-9	☐ 6	☐ 17-19
7.	☐ 8:48-59	☐ 3:10-18	☐ 7	☐ 20-21
		▸ **1 JOHN**		
8.	☐ 9:1-12	☐ 1:1-4	☐ 8	☐ 22-23
9.	☐ 9:13-25	☐ 1:5-10	☐ 9:1-20	☐ 24-26
10.	☐ 9:26-41	☐ 2:1-11	☐ 9:21-35	☐ 27-28
11.	☐ 10:1-10	☐ 2:12-17	☐ 10	☐ 29-30
12.	☐ 10:11-21	☐ 2:18-23	☐ 11	☐ 31-32
13.	☐ 10:22-42	☐ 2:24-29	☐ 12	☐ 33-34
14.	☐ 11:1-16	☐ 3:1-10	☐ 13	☐ 35-37
15.	☐ 11:17-37	☐ 3:11-18	☐ 14	☐ 38-39
16.	☐ 11:38-44	☐ 3:19-24	☐ 15:1-16	☐ 40-41
17.	☐ 11:45-57	☐ 4:1-6	☐ 15:17-35	☐ 42-44
18.	☐ 12:1-11	☐ 4:7-21	☐ 16	☐ 45-47
19.	☐ 12:12-19	☐ 5:1-12	☐ 17	☐ 48
				▸ **DANIEL**
20.	☐ 12:20-36	☐ 5:13-21	☐ 18	☐ 1-2
		▸ **2 JOHN**		
21.	☐ 12:37-50	☐ 1-13	☐ 19	☐ 3-4
		▸ **3 JOHN**		
22.	☐ 13:1-11	☐ 1-14	☐ 20	☐ 5-6
		▸ **JUDE**		
23.	☐ 13:12-17	☐ 1-7	☐ 21:1-21	☐ 7-8
24.	☐ 13:18-30	☐ 8-16	☐ 21:22-34	☐ 9
25.	☐ 13:31-38	☐ 17-25	☐ 22	☐ 10-12

December

	New Testament		Old Testament	
	▸ JOHN	▸ REVELATION	▸ JOB	▸ HOSEA
1.	☐ 14:1-14	☐ 1:1-8	☐ 23	☐ 1-3
2.	☐ 14:15-21	☐ 1:9-20	☐ 24	☐ 4-6
3.	☐ 14:22-31	☐ 2:1-17	☐ 25-26	☐ 7-8
4.	☐ 15:1-8	☐ 2:18-29	☐ 27	☐ 9-12
5.	☐ 15:9-17	☐ 3:1-13	☐ 28	☐ 13-14
				▸ JOEL
6.	☐ 15:18-27	☐ 3:14-22	☐ 29	☐ 1
7.	☐ 16:1-11	☐ 4	☐ 30	☐ 2-3
				▸ AMOS
8.	☐ 16:12-24	☐ 5	☐ 31:1-23	☐ 1-2
9.	☐ 16:25-33	☐ 6	☐ 31:24-40	☐ 3-4
10.	☐ 17:1-5	☐ 7	☐ 32	☐ 5-6
11.	☐ 17:6-19	☐ 8	☐ 33:1-11	☐ 7-9
				▸ OBADIAH
12.	☐ 17:20-26	☐ 9	☐ 33:12-33	☐ 1-21
				▸ JONAH
13.	☐ 18:1-18	☐ 10	☐ 34:1-20	☐ 1-4
				▸ MICAH
14.	☐ 18:19-27	☐ 11	☐ 34:21-37	☐ 1-3
15.	☐ 18:28-40	☐ 12	☐ 35	☐ 4-5
16.	☐ 19:1-16	☐ 13	☐ 36:1-15	☐ 6-7
				▸ NAHUM
17.	☐ 19:17-27	☐ 14	☐ 36:16-33	☐ 1-3
				▸ HABAKKUK
18.	☐ 19:28-37	☐ 15	☐ 37	☐ 1-3
				▸ ZEPHANIAH
19.	☐ 19:38-42	☐ 16	☐ 38:1-21	☐ 1-2
20.	☐ 20:1-9	☐ 17	☐ 38:22-41	☐ 3
				▸ HAGGAI
21.	☐ 20:10-18	☐ 18	☐ 39	☐ 1-2
				▸ ZECHARIAH
22.	☐ 20:19-23	☐ 19	☐ 40	☐ 1-5
23.	☐ 20:24-31	☐ 20	☐ 41:1-11	☐ 6-9
24.	☐ 21:1-14	☐ 21	☐ 41:12-34	☐ 10-14
				▸ MALACHI
25.	☐ 21:15-25	☐ 22	☐ 42	☐ 1-4

Also by Steve Uppal

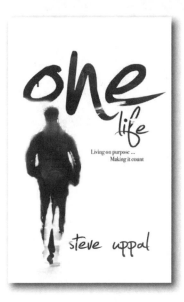

ONE LIFE – *Living on Purpose; Making it Count.* Life is a gift we have all been given. Each of us only gets one shot at it – one chance to make the most of it and to make a difference in our world. God has given us one life – how will you live yours? This book unpacks the principles of living a life of purpose, helping us to identify and understand our calling and explaining the difference between the purpose that is true for all believers and our individual, unique purpose in Christ.

ROUSING THE WARRIORS – *A prophetic call to rise up and boldly advance the kingdom of God.* All over the world God is speaking to His Church and calling her to rise up, take her rightful place and be all He has called her to be. This book will stir believers to find their place in God's plan and engage with His purposes for them. It will help equip an end-time army for the battles that lie ahead.

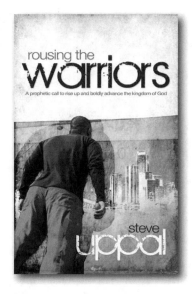